Many Voices, One People

Reflections on the Book of Genesis by Hofstra University Hillel Staff, Alumni, and Friends

**Edited by
Rabbi Meir Mitelman**

Hofstra
Hillel
The Center for Jewish Life on Campus

ISBN: 978-1-7322104-1-7

Table of Contents

Greetings

The reflections in these pages are a powerful example of what Hofstra Hillel: The Foundation for Jewish Campus Life has been doing for 70 years – bringing individuals together in a dynamic community to explore and celebrate their Jewish heritage.

There are many contributors to this project – alumni, faculty, staff, and community partners. Each of them has felt the impact of Hofstra Hillel's work, and in response they have contributed not only their words, but their actions as well. They have helped to create a vibrant, welcoming Jewish "home" within the large and diverse community that is Hofstra University.

College is a time for students to open their minds and their hearts to new ideas and experiences. From weekly Shabbat activities and thought-provoking speakers to solemn rituals such as their Six Hours for the Six Million – the annual reading of the names of Jewish children who were killed in concentration camps – to commemorate Holocaust Remembrance Day, Hofstra Hillel has enriched and educated the entire campus community.

Several years ago Hofstra Hillel brought "Ask Big Questions" to our campus. This important fellowship program is an award-winning initiative which brings students together, regardless of faith, race, ethnicity, gender identity, sexual orientation, or political beliefs, to discuss challenging issues from the everyday to universal questions about existence and our role in the world.

Hofstra Hillel also has an enthusiastic commitment to community service, with student participation in Alternative Winter and Spring Break service projects, frequent visits with senior adults, and the annual campus-wide Thanks & Giving Project which encourages all members of the university community to write personalized cards expressing appreciation to fellow students, faculty, staff, and administration for their work.

The energy and enthusiasm members of Hofstra Hillel bring to their organization is extraordinary. Its students – smart, caring, community-minded young people – are always looking for new ways to integrate Jewish values into their activities and to make a difference in the lives of others.

This book is another example of the creativity and innovative spirit that drives Hofstra Hillel. That so many have come together to participate in this project is testament to the lasting impact this important organization has had on their lives, on our campus, and on the Long Island Jewish community.

Stuart Rabinowitz
President, Hofstra University

Foreword

I proudly welcome the publication of this book of Torah, *Many Voices, One People: Reflections on the Book of Genesis by Hofstra University Hillel Staff, Alumni, and Friends* by my colleagues at Hofstra Hillel.

Hillel is committed to "inspiring every Jewish student to make an enduring commitment to Jewish life, learning and Israel." A vibrant Hillel on campus is more than a "home away from home." It is a place where the emerging leaders of the Jewish community begin to define their own Jewish identities. At Hillel, they gain the confidence to participate in all the obligations, joys and rituals of Jewish life on their own terms, not just as a member of the family in which they were raised.

Nothing is more fundamental to the development of a strong Jewish identity than a comfort and familiarity with Torah study, and an understanding of how Torah has shaped Jewish life throughout history and continues to yield new insights that help us live meaningful lives today. It is essential that today's students understand that they can apply their own intellect and experience to Torah study and interpretation, adding their ideas to the long line of commentary that has shaped our people.

With the publication of this volume, Hofstra Hillel demonstrates to another generation of young Jews that *Lo bashamayim hi*, the Torah is not in the heavens, but right here on earth for us to learn, interpret and teach.

I want to offer my special congratulations to Rabbi Dave Siegel, the executive director of Hofstra Hillel, and Rabbi Meir Mitelman, the executive director emeritus, for their inspired leadership in imagining, organizing, and producing this volume.

Rabbis Siegel and Mitelman are exemplars among the teachers of Torah that Hillel is fortunate to have working on more than 600 campuses and locations in 17 countries throughout the world. Their gentle but determined approach to sustaining vibrant Jewish life at Hofstra University has made an impact on countless lives and has truly helped sustain the Jewish people. For this, they have my deepest respect and gratitude.

Eytz chayim hi lamachazikim ba. Torah is a tree of life to those who hold it fast. *Many Voices, One People* adds another beautiful leaf to the countless branches of Torah study. On behalf of the entire Hillel movement, *Kol Hakavod* to Hofstra Hillel!

Eric Fingerhut
President & CEO, Hillel International
Washington, DC
June 2017

Preface

As the Executive Director it is my pleasure to present *Many Voices, One People: Reflections on the Book of Genesis*. This volume epitomizes the work that Hofstra University Hillel has been doing for more than 70 years, bringing individuals together to learn from one another and to explore their Jewish identities. Hillel means different things to different people. Whether it is attending our weekly Shabbat dinners, traveling to Israel, discussing politics, playing sports, singing in our *a cappella* group Chai Notes, working as an intern, or simply hanging out in the office, each of these things plays an essential role in our mission: enriching the lives of Jewish students so that they may enrich the Jewish people and the world.

This project highlights two important aspects of Hofstra University Hillel. The first is an acknowledgement of the strength of our pluralistic approach to Jewish life. Although the voices that appear in these reflections may have different approaches to understanding God, Jewish law, Jewish texts, and Jewish peoplehood, there is no doubt that we are still members of one people, one community. In a world fraught with division, it is essential that we serve as an example that individuals holding different opinions can learn, celebrate, and grow together. As it states in the Talmud when referring to the debate between the Schools of Hillel and Shammai, "*eilu v'eilu divrei Elokim hayim,*" "Both these and those are the words of the living God." (Eiruvin 13b).

A second important aspect of this project is our choice to focus on *parashat hashavua*, the weekly Torah reading. At the heart of everything we do at Hofstra University Hillel is Jewish learning. No matter your understanding of its origins, it is the Torah, our core foundation text, that binds us together as a people. It is our job to study it, struggle with it, and even challenge it. My hope is that this volume will provide a starting point for all members of our community, those new to studying Jewish texts and those who have been exposed to these words for their entire lives. Each has something to say to add to this conversation.

This book could not have been completed without the vision, hard work, and patience of two very important individuals: our editors, Rabbi Meir Mitelman and Dorrie Berkowitz. Rabbi Meir, better known as Rabs, has been inspiring Jewish students for over forty years. Whether it is his weekly classes or informal conversations,

Rabbi Meir inspires us to learn more about our tradition and ourselves. His impact is clear throughout this book. Although this was the first time Dorrie has worked with our community, there is no doubt that she is part of the *mispacha* (family). Her professionalism, creativity, laughter, and most of all her patience have ensured not only that this book would be completed, but that it truly reflects the *neshama*, the soul, of Hofstra University Hillel. I would also like to thank our partners, Hofstra University, Hillel International, and UJA Federation of New York. You are all essential to the work we are doing, both on campus and in the greater Long Island community. Everything we accomplish is due to your support.

Thank you to all of the students, staff, and board members who have been part of Hofstra University Hillel. The voices of this book are your voices. Although we may have not met personally, you are clearly part of the chain of thoughts and actions that are dedicated to supporting our students and making this world a better place.

Last, but not least, I would like to thank my family, specifically my wife and children. Thank you for welcoming Hofstra students into our home and into our lives. You are an important part of the work we do.

Each day I am blessed with interacting with members of our community. Students, staff, alumni, and community members each with unique backgrounds and perspectives. The content of this book is a sample of the the amazing conversations that occur in our office every day. Our hope is that the reflections in these pages will inspire each of us to continue discussing the words of our tradition whether you are in the Hillel lounge, drinking coffee in a cafe in Israel, or resting comfortably in your living room.

Rabbi Dave Siegel
Executive Director, Hofstra University Hillel
Hofstra University Jewish Chaplain

Introduction

When Rabbi Dave Siegel, Hofstra Hillel's executive director, first shared with me his idea to publish a book of *d'vrei Torah* by a variety of people who are – or have been – part of Hofstra Hillel's community, I immediately thought "Great idea!" I was even more excited when Rabbi Dave suggested I be the project director.

As we discussed basic issues regarding the book, we agreed the contributors should be people who have a variety of relationships with Hofstra Hillel. We also agreed the *d'vrei Torah* should reflect the wide range of perspectives on Jewish theology, law, and observance. This decision was essential to ensure that this project represents the broad spectrum of people and ideas fundamental to all Hillels. The result is the Book of Genesis, the first volume of this unique project, *Many Voices, One People*. Rabbi Dave and I envision publishing additional volumes, one for each of the remaining Five Books of Moses, and each based on the same principle of pluralism.

Many people have made this innovative project possible. I am, of course, deeply grateful for all the contributors who accepted our invitation to write one, two, or three *d'vrei Torah* for this book. One aspect of the project I treasured was connecting with Hofstra Hillel alumni, colleagues both present and past, and friends of our Hillel, all of whom have made a meaningful difference for Hofstra Hillel and have been an inspiration to me.

I want to express my gratitude to Rabbi Dave for his support and invaluable feedback. With his visionary, creative leadership, our Hillel continues to grow with exciting initiatives, quality programs, student participation, and high energy. Becca Schwartzberg (Hofstra, 2017), a student intern at our Hillel (and now on Hillel's staff at Tulane University), played a major role in proofing the articles, developing the glossary, and much more. I am thankful for all her very helpful work.

The president of Hofstra University, Stuart Rabinowitz, is a good friend of Hofstra Hillel. Several years ago he was honored with the Hillel Award at our annual dinner. Throughout all the years since he became president in June 2001, President Rabinowitz's devoted support of our Hillel has truly made a difference in the work we do. For all that and more, my colleagues at our Hillel, our students, and our Board of Directors are deeply thankful.

Eric Fingerhut is Hillel International's Director and CEO. His inspiring leadership includes an innovative strategic plan for all Hillels that focuses on helping more and more Jewish students make an enduring commitment to Jewish life, learning, and Israel. For all that, and for his genial manner, enthusiastic support, and more, all of us at Hofstra Hillel are greatly appreciative.

My dear friends, Drs. Nechama and William Liss-Levinson (both published authors), enthusiastically said "yes" when I asked them to brainstorm with me about different aspects of this book. I am very thankful for their gracious, creative input, some of it incorporated in these pages.

With his many years of experience, Alan Mitelman, winner of numerous awards in graphic design, is responsible for the layout and design of this project. He has devoted a great deal of time not only to the aesthetics of this book, but also to editorial suggestions. For his dedicated commitment to excellence, I am deeply grateful.

Dorrie Berkowitz, our editor for this book, has been a professional editor for many decades. She has devoted a great deal of time to this project, amidst many other responsibilities. Her experience over the years, along with her patience, careful editing, sense of humor, speedy response to my emails and voicemails, and enthusiastic dedication are only a few things that have made it a joy and a wonderful learning experience working with her. I especially appreciate her generosity of spirit in advising me both about the basics of publishing a book and about some challenging issues during the process of publishing this book. For all the above and more, my heartfelt thanks.

Whether these *d'vrei Torah* are a source for teaching, a springboard for lively discussions with others, and/or some fresh interpretations for a reader to ponder in solitude, I, along with my colleagues and the contributors, hope these creative and often personal insights on the Book of Genesis will be enriching and inspiring. May these reflections on the first book of the Torah evoke a thirst to explore Jewish texts, learn about our Jewish heritage, and understand how they speak to us today.

Rabbi Meir Mitelman
Director of Community Outreach, Hofstra University Hillel
Executive Director Emeritus, Hofstra University Hillel

Note to Readers

Translations and Transliterations
The translations and transliterations from Hebrew to English are subjective tasks. In this Hofstra Hillel volume of Torah commentary, the respellings may seem inconsistent. However, a conscious decision was made to reflect source materials, commonly accepted forms for familiar words, and other historical or traditional criteria rather than to impose a rigid format. In addition, the editors respected the translations in each contributor's work.

Glossary
This Hofstra Hillel Torah commentary was created to serve readers of all backgrounds and at all levels of obervance. The glossary is not meant to be comprehensive but rather to function as a foundation for understanding.

Dorrie Berkowitz
Managing Editor

בראשית

B'reishit

Keeping Your Balance

Rabbi Dr. Ronald L. Androphy

The primary issue cosmologists debate is "How was the universe created?" Currently, the "Big Bang Theory" is the dominant hypothesis for the genesis of the universe; it posits an initial explosion that yields an ever-expanding world. From time to time, other theories have suggested the opposite.

Interestingly, several second-century CE rabbis debated the same issue (see Babylonian Talmud, *Yoma* 54b). Rabbi Eliezer claimed that "the world was created from its center"; in other words, the world was created from the inside out. Rabbi Joshua, on the other hand, suggested that "the world was created from the sides," *i.e.*, from the outside in. I do not think that Rabbi Eliezer and Rabbi Joshua were debating science; in my opinion, they were arguing over the nature of the world and human experience. For Rabbi Eliezer the world was created by a process of expansion. For him – and for us as well – the world was constantly expanding.

Rabbi Eliezer lived at a time of Greek and Roman influence and domination. Along with their armies, the Greeks and Romans brought their culture and their arts, their philosophies, their literature, and their scientific methods to relatively provincial Palestine. Immediately, the Jew's world expanded: New ways of thinking, new methods of study, new subjects of study, new opportunities for achievement, new sources of leisure became available. His formerly circumscribed world practically exploded, opening vistas and horizons never even dreamt of before. Indeed, the world had expanded.

And so it continues to do for us today. Just think of how much the world has expanded in the past twenty years! The ubiquity of computers, the internet, social media; new discoveries in science, medicine, and technology; pioneering work in the fields of education, psychology, even archaeology all expand our minds, our knowledge, and our universe. Rabbi Eliezer was correct: Our world is constantly expanding!

But the world's expansion is not always for the good. I am certain that Rabbi Eliezer saw the negative aspects of an expanding world: people growing apart, the breakdown of families and societies, the destruction of community spirit, a growing divisiveness and factionalism among the Jewish people, more Jews drifting away from their Jewish heritage.

What Rabbi Eliezer saw in his world we see in ours as well. How many families are there today in which the parents, children, and grandchildren live in the same community? Is there any Jewish community that has not been impacted by the by-products of our expanding world: assimilation and intermarriage? And, as we read constantly in the news, are not nations growing further and further apart? Yes, the world is expanding, but not always for the better.

On the other hand, for Rabbi Joshua, who claimed that the world was created from the outside in, the world was created by a process of contraction. For Rabbi Joshua – and for us – the world was constantly shrinking.

How correct Rabbi Joshua was! Thanks to better methods of transportation and communication, we can reach just about any point on the globe in less than a day; we can call any telephone in the world and speak with near-crystal clarity; we can watch in real time practically any event that is occurring at any given moment even in the most remote part of the world; thanks to social media we can share our feelings, sentiments, and good or bad news with millions of people instantaneously; thanks to the internet we can converse in milliseconds with people thousands of miles away. Our world definitely has shrunk.

But our world has contracted in a negative sense as well. It has contracted in such a way that on all too many occasions individuals feel alone, feel that the world has closed in on them, feel that they are a part of nothing meaningful. Perhaps at no other time in human history have so many people felt alone, despite the connectiveness of social media, and perhaps because of its destructive potential. This is manifest in numerous ways: high rates of depression, the intolerably high number of young people attempting suicide, the threats posed by "lone wolves," the number of people "bowling alone." Yes, as Rabbi Joshua posited, the world is shrinking, but not always for the better.

So how does a Jew maintain his/her balance in a world that is constantly expanding and contracting, both positively and negatively? The answer may lie in the third Talmudic answer to the question "How was the world created?"

Unlike Rabbi Eliezer who claimed that the world was created from the inside out, and differing from Rabbi Joshua who maintained that the world was created from the outside in, the Sages claimed, "the world was created from Zion outward."

For the Sages, Zion represents Torah: "For from Zion shall go forth the Law, and the word of the Lord from Jerusalem" (Is. 2:3). The Sages are intimating that for the Jew the world begins with Torah, the word of God. Adherence to our Jewish heritage, our Jewish values, and our Jewish way of life lies at the center of our existence, and, like a beacon, Torah casts forth its light from Zion and illumines the proper path for us as we steer our course past the shoals and breakers of an expanding and contrasting world. By grabbing hold of Torah, by studying its teachings, by observing its precepts, and by embracing its values, the Jew will find his balance in the world and will be able to withstand the uneven tides of a conflicted world.

"The Torah is a tree of life" – a life preserver in the ebb and flow of a chaotic world – "to all who grab hold of it" (Prov. 3:18).

Seeing the Divine

Rabbi Bruce Bromberg Seltzer

*P*arashat B'reishit is literally the beginning. In it, God creates the world and all it contains. While it starts out about the creation of the universe, the Torah is a story for and about people. The *parasha* focuses on the first generations of humans, narrowing from the creation of humanity in the first chapters to the emergence of distinct people. By the end, the *parasha* focuses on one family, that of Abraham.

While the *parasha* contains many of the most well-known events in the Torah, one lesser-known passage, Genesis 5:1, is worthy of attention: "This is the book of the lineage of Adam: On the day God created the human, in the image of God He created him."[1]

This verse introduces us to humanity from its first member, Adam, through his descendants over its first generations. It contains more than an introduction to Adam's extended family, since it adds "in the image of God He created him." Since the Torah already told us when Adam was first created that he was created in the image of God, why is this repeated?

A midrash examining a famous verse in Leviticus, "and you shall love your fellow as yourself" (Lev.19:18), offers a possible answer for Genesis 5:1 repeating that Adam is created in God's image. "Rabbi Akiva said: This Leviticus 19:18 is a primary principle of Torah. Ben Azzai said: the verse in Genesis 5:1 'This is the book of the Generations of Adam...' is more of a primary principle than that." Rabbi Akiva's choice of the Leviticus verse as a primary principle makes sense; it offers an ethical approach to dealing with other people as one would want to be treated. In contrast, the differences between the verses help explain Ben Azzai's choice of our verse in Genesis as a primary principle.

The ethical principle in Rabbi Akiva's selection from Leviticus is based on our relationship to a specific individual – "your fellow." The verses' context in Leviticus 19:17-18 is the complexities of interpersonal relationships (focusing on reproach, revenge, and grudges). In such a case, a person's relationship with individuals or their actions might make it difficult to love them as one loves oneself. Furthermore, at times we might not love ourselves. These explanations of the Leviticus verse raise questions about it being a primary principle of the Torah.

Our Genesis verse does not directly discuss interpersonal relationships and ethics, so Ben Azzai must be focusing on the repeated information that humans are made in the Divine image when he selects it as a primary principle. Although the midrash does not state it explicitly, most commentators interpret his statement as saying that the primary principle is to remember that everyone is created in God's image. Considering everyone we encounter (or even those we never meet who may be affected by our actions or by the political and economic choices we make in our daily lives) as equally made in the Divine image changes the way we relate to other people. We learn to treat everyone equitably and fairly. This idea contrasts to Akiva's narrower selection of a verse based on a fellow, a person near you or with whom you have a relationship.

It is hard to view some people as having been created in the Divine image. Sometimes I don't, especially people different from me or with whom I have a disagreement. Still, imagine some of the possible implications: Drivers during bad traffic might be less aggressive if they consciously thought of every other driver as a driver created in the Divine image; politicians might make more inclusive and kind choices if they actively thought that each person affected by legislation is equally made in the Divine image; or people would give more generously to panhandlers if they considered that the person asking them is made in the Divine image.

While the implications for us as individuals are impressive, the implications on society and our planet could be massive if applied broadly.

Judaism views each of us as a microcosm of the world. Ben Azzai's use of the verse as a primary principle of the Torah (especially in comparison to Akiva's verse) implies that we should relate in the same way to everyone we meet and who may be affected by our actions.

So, the next time someone cuts you off in the cafeteria or upsets you with a crass remark, remember that Ben Azzai teaches us to view everyone in the Divine image.

---

[1] Alter, Robert. *The Five Books of Moses: A Translation with Commentary*. New York: WW Norton, 2004.

In the Beginning –
Creating Identity

Hanita Wishnevski

Clothes make the man. Naked people have little or no influence on society.
Mark Twain

Clothes may not alter the essential nature of a person, but can alter the way others perceive that person. If a professor showed up to teach in his pajamas or her evening gown, students may not give as much credence to what was being taught as they might if the professor came to class looking "professorial." While this may seem shallow or unfair, and while "professorial" attire differs in different cultures, human beings tend to make judgments based on external criteria such as appearance, and not on internal qualities such as character. Apparently, what we see with our eyes often trumps what we are capable of "seeing" with our brains.

According to Jewish belief, God has no physical form and therefore has no sartorial issues. Then what is meant in Genesis, Chapter 1:26: "And God said, 'Let us make man in our image, after our likeness,'" and in Chapter 1:27: "And God created man in His image, in the image of God He created him; male and female He created them."

It appears that the first person was created half male and half female, representing the "image" of God, and was then separated into two beings: one male and one female. Somehow, over the centuries, and the interpretations of overwhelmingly male commentators, God's creation became "man" and his subordinate help-mate "woman."

Looking at the root of *tzelem*, generally translated as "image," is perhaps better rendered as "shadow." A shadow connotes an absence of details, leaving an outline, a form, a no-thingness, that remains to be filled. Human beings were God's only creation created in God's image, in the no-thingness that is God, created to flesh out God's work, and who also have the capacity to continue the work of creation.

To be created in someone's image or shadow can also mean to imitate the creator, to follow in his/her footsteps, to duplicate his/her function, to have an identity created for you. What do we know about God at the time of creation? Chapter 1 of Genesis tells us that on days one through five, God created the heavens and the earth, the seas, vegetation and animals primarily by "speaking" or "naming" them into existence, and that God found it good. The act of creation itself can be viewed as God's imposing order on chaos by separating one thing from another (light from darkness, dry land from water), bringing new life forms (vegetation, animals) into existence, and creating identities for these entities.

On day six, God creates humankind. As we saw in Chapter 1, woman and man are created together, both in God's image. In the second creation story in Chapter 2, God forms man from dust; breathes life into him; plants trees in the Garden of Eden; forms all the wild animals and birds out of the earth; brings them to the man to name; forms woman from the man's side and brings her to the man to name. It is only at the time that they decide to eat the fruit of the tree of knowledge of good and evil[1] that Adam and the woman, like most children, start to forge their individual identities, contrary to their parent's (God's) perception of them. They have free will; they can choose.

After the fruit-eating incident, God punishes his creations/children for disobeying the parental instructions, Adam names the woman Chava (Eve), God provides clothing for Adam and Chava before expelling Adam from the Garden of Eden. Interestingly, the text contains no mention that Chava was also evicted, although she apparently goes with Adam. Chava gives birth to Cain and Abel, and we are told that she names Cain. Later, Chava gives birth to Seth and names him too.

What is the significance of naming something or someone? Naming is not only a creative act, but it also implies that the one naming has some understanding, knowledge, control, and/or power over the named. Naming can also be limiting. Once something (or someone) is named, it as though a box has been drawn around it and its identity is contained within those lines. Throughout our lives, we collect many names: the names given to us at birth, nicknames, titular or professional names, names pertaining to our perceived stature or reputation, and so on. Just as with clothes, these names may define how others view us as well as how we view ourselves. Our names often precede us, and instead of being understood as a whole, complex being with the entire panoply of human capabilities and emotions, we are identified as homeless, astrophysicist, grandma, geek, orphan, drama queen, Murgatroyd, and treated according to whatever expectations such names generate in others.

On the other hand, to be without a name is akin to not existing. How does one make real, identify another person without a name? Where does that leave God? What does it mean when people "name" God?

According to Jewish teaching, God is not knowable, has no form, yet human beings have given God names, identified God, implying a knowledge of and control over God, while simultaneously limiting our understanding of God.

Yet, without a name, how would God "exist" for us? When not reading Torah or praying, it is common among some Jews to refer to God as *Hashem*, which translates to "The Name." Arguably, this designation is more indicative of God's "no-thingness," God's image or identity.

Although identified by various appellations throughout our lives, perhaps the most important identity that we humans have is the "name" that conveys the "content of [our] character"[2], the "name" that we will be remembered for, the "name" which we leave behind.

---

[1] In the biblical story, before the creation of the woman from Adam's side, God explicitly tells Adam not to eat from that tree. Later on, Adam is next to the woman when the snake extols the benefits of eating from the tree, but Adam says nothing of God's earlier warning. Instead he partakes of the fruit when the woman gives him some.

[2] The Rev. Dr. Martin Luther King, Jr., "I Have a Dream" speech at Lincoln Memorial, Washington Mall, Aug. 28, 1963.

נח

—

Noaḥ

Opening Your Eyes

Rabbi Dr. Ronald L. Androphy

*P*arashat *Noah* contains the famous and familiar story of
Noah and the Flood. Mankind had become so violent and
corrupt that God decided to destroy the world that He had
created. He instructed Noah, the only righteous man, to
construct an ark, a tillerless ship, and to take into the ark his family
and representative samples of all species of animal life. God informed
Noah that He was about to bring a flood that would destroy all of
mankind; only those in the ark would survive. Noah constructed
the ark, brought in his family and the animals, and the deluge began.
It rained for forty days and forty nights; all life was decimated.

How high did the waters of the Flood rise? The book of Genesis
supplies the answer: "When the waters had swelled and increased
greatly upon the earth, all the highest mountains everywhere under
the sky were covered. Fifteen cubits higher did the waters swell,
as the mountains were covered" (Gen. 7:19-20).

While the answer to the question about how high the Flood waters
rose seems pretty straightforward – the waters climbed 15 cubits
(approximately 22.5 feet) above the mountains – two Talmudic rabbis
disagreed as to the interpretation of these verses from Genesis 7.
Rabbi Yehudah claimed that the verse meant, "Fifteen cubits above
the mountains and fifteen cubits above the plains." Rabbi Nehemiah,
however, maintained that the waters rose "Fifteen cubits above the
mountains, and whatever that turns out to be above the plains."

Do you realize the difference between the two suggestions?

According to Rabbi Yehudah, the waters of the Flood rose to a height
of fifteen cubits above any given geological formation. To illustrate:
The Himalayas rise approximately 29,000 feet above sea level;
according to Rabbi Yehudah, that means that the waters of the Flood
climbed to a height of 29,000 feet +15 cubits in Nepal and Tibet.
The Rocky Mountains reach a height of about 14,000 feet; Rabbi
Yehudah would say that in the western United States the waters of
the Flood stood at 14,000 feet +15 cubits. Hofstra University rests on
the Hempstead Plain, which lies 50 feet above sea level; the Flood
did not reach even 100 feet here on Long Island. The Dead Sea lies
at almost 1,000 feet below sea level; Rabbi Yehudah would claim
that there the Flood waters rose to 975 feet below sea level. Just think
about this arrangement; it is physically impossible! Water cannot

maintain its position at different levels in the same container (here, the earth); water always flows downward until it becomes level on a surface.

Rabbi Nehemiah interprets the verses the same way human experience dictates. If the waters of the Flood rose to a height of 15 cubits above the highest mountains, that meant that over the Himalayas they were 29,000 feet +15 cubits; 15,000 feet +15 cubits above the Rockies (for a total height of 29,022 feet); 28,950 feet +15 cubits above Hofstra (for a total height of 29,022 feet); and 30,000 feet +15 cubits above the Dead Sea (for a total height of 29,022 feet). The waters throughout the world were at the same level: 29,000 feet +15 cubits.

Why this difference in interpretation between Rabbi Yehudah and Rabbi Nehemiah? How could Rabbi Yehudah possibly claim that the waters were uneven across the surface of the earth? Didn't he realize that that is a physical impossibility?

I think the answer to these questions reflects the difference in attitudes and outlooks between the two rabbis. Rabbi Nehemiah looked out at the world and saw regularity and sameness. He perceived that the normal patterns of nature continued undisturbed; he saw nothing special in nature, nothing unusual. For him the world was unchanging, even monotonous. He would agree with the words of Ecclesiastes: "One generation goes, another comes, but the earth remains the same forever...There is nothing new under the sun" (Eccles. 1:4,9).

Rabbi Yehudah, on the other hand, views nature as varied. He sees the physical world as full of differences and gradations; he detects the beauty in – and he celebrates – the constantly changing patterns of nature. For him, the physical world consists of an endless series of daily miracles.

Where Rabbi Nehemiah perceives sameness and monotony, Rabbi Yehudah detects beauty; where Rabbi Nehemiah sees nothing unusual, Rabbi Yehudah finds miracles!

It seems to me that more and more we are adopting the attitude of Rabbi Nehemiah rather than that of Rabbi Yehudah. In our age of technology, mass production, rampant commercialism, and conspicuous consumption we are losing our appreciation of the beauty in the world around us. We are losing our ability to perceive the beauty, wonder, and miraculous quality of the beautiful world God has created for us. Like Rabbi Nehemiah, we look out and see sameness, evenness, and monotony in nature.

We build cities, and block out our view of the sky and the heavens.

We build metropolises, and we destroy forests, wetlands, and farmlands.

We fill in streams.

We change the course of rivers.

We pollute our water and air.

We create so much smog that on some days it is impossible to see nearby hills and mountains.

We level everything and create a dull uniformity.

We dull our own appreciation of nature and the beauty of God's universe.

Ask yourself: When was the last time you:

- looked at the stars at night (if you could even see them!)? gazed at a full moon? stopped to appreciate a sunset?

- marveled at a rainbow?

- paused in awe – not in fear – during a thunderstorm?

- spent a day basking in fall foliage?

Many of us don't bother.

Most of us don't take the time to do so.

All too many of us don't care.

What a shame to lose the ability to stand in awe, enveloped in a sense of wonder at the beauty of the world that God has created for us! What a shame not to appreciate the miracle that is nature! As the Baal Shem Tov, the founder of Hasidism said, "The world is full of wonders and miracles, but man takes his little hand and covers his eyes and sees nothing."

We must adopt the attitude toward the world that is reflected in Rabbi Yehudah's interpretation of the verses from Genesis 27: The world is a miracle! In fact, Judaism sees the world as full of so many miracles that we have blessings that we are to say when we see or experience such natural phenomena as lightning, thunder, earthquakes, comets, mountains, rivers, rainbows, and even especially beautiful people and unusual creatures. We must sensitize ourselves to detect the beauty in nature. We must realize that this world – and our lives – are truly miraculous gifts from God!

Comforting
Heaven and Earth

Gittel Marcus

Noah is introduced in the Torah at the end of the first *parasha,*
B'reishit: Lameh lived one hundred and eighty-two years,
and begot a son. And he called his name "Noah," saying,
"This one will bring us rest from our work and from the toil
of our hands, from the ground which God had cursed.

> When Noah was five hundred years old, Noah begot Shem,
> Ham and Japheth....
>
> God saw that the wickedness of Man was great upon the earth,
> and that every product of the thoughts of his heart was but
> evil always. And God reconsidered having made Man on earth,
> and He had heartfelt sadness. And God said, "I will blot out
> Man whom I created from the face of the ground – from man
> to animal, to creeping things, and to birds of the sky; for I have
> reconsidered My having made them." But Noah found grace
> in the eyes of God....(Gen. 6:5 – 8).

Lameh seems to have put much faith in Noah as a redeemer.
"This one will bring us rest from our work," he says, which seems to
indicate that he along with others saw Noah as some kind of hero
who would make their lives easier. The next *parasha, Parashat Noah,*
begins with a similar compliment of Noah, but from God:
"...Noah was a righteous man, perfect in his generations; Noah
walked with God."

Did Noah meet any of these promises in his lifetime? While the text
describes righteousness, but doesn't specify what Noah did, midrash
has filled in some of the details: Noah invented plows, sickles,
axes, and all kinds of tools, thus freeing humanity from "the toil of
their hands," as Lameh had said. And did Noah deserve to be called
righteous? Well, he did do as God asked, exactly as God asked.

But this wasn't enough. Still the Flood came, and everything was
destroyed except for Noah and his family (and the animals and
plants that Noah had rescued on his ark). Noah's righteousness
wasn't enough to avert the decree, to save everything, but it was
enough to save a remnant. Thanks to Noah, a part of the world
had been preserved.

With the passage of time, and with the subsequent lessons of Abraham and Moses, we tend to judge Noaḥ by what he didn't do. He should have warned others around him to repent; he should have argued with God on behalf of humanity's potential. As Rabbi Jonathan Sacks writes, "[God] seeks from us something other and greater than obedience, namely responsibility." And in this respect, Noaḥ failed.

In *Parashat Noaḥ*, God tells Noaḥ to "Make for yourself an ark of gopher wood" (Gen. 6:14). Rabbi Moshe Alshich, a rabbi who lived in the 16th century in Tzfat, comments that the text "make for yourself" means that God was actually saying to Noaḥ "Make an ark to symbolize your own behavior. You remained aloof from your compatriots instead of chastising them and trying to save them by improving their conduct. Now, you will isolate yourself in an ark with the beasts and the animals."

Rabbi Jonathan Sacks writes that the story of Noaḥ is part of a "developmental line in the narrative of the evolution of humanity." In the Garden of Eden they were concerned primarily for their own welfare, not so much for those around them. Eve enticed Adam to eat of the tree of knowledge, then both hid from God, and then blamed each other. Cain murdered Abel and upon God confronting him with his crime declared, "Am I my brother's keeper?" Lameh upon the birth of his child Noaḥ basically declared, "May this child make our lives easier."

Noaḥ is different. He helps his generation, according to what they most desired: an easier life. He is obedient to God in an age that lost total regard for anything holy. Noaḥ is the first character in the Torah to realize that his life has a greater purpose than his own personal wants and desires, the first to realize that he is a part of a brotherhood of humanity (the creation of the tools and the plows), and part of the heavenly design (the dedication to the will of God).

It's true, he didn't go far enough: He did not help his fellow men become better than they were, nor did he fight for the potential of what they could be. Abraham was the one who introduced those ideas, and it was he who became the patriarch of the Jewish people.

What does this mean for Noaḥ's legacy? A comment by R. Isaiah di Trani, an Italian Talmud scholar, offers a parable, which can apply to Noaḥ as well.

> ...A wise philosopher: "Who sees further, a dwarf or a giant? Surely a giant, for his eyes are situated at a higher level than those of the dwarf. But if the dwarf is placed on the shoulders

*of the giant who sees further?...So too we are dwarfs astride
the shoulders of giants. We master their wisdom and move
beyond it. Due to their wisdom we grow wise and are able to
say all that we say, but not because we are greater than they."*

But Noah's value isn't only that he allowed Abraham to go further
in moral development. If that were the case, why bother including
his story at all in the Torah? Why not just start with the first one who
really got it right?

With the *parashiyot* of *B'reishit* and of *Noah*, before *Lekh Lekha*,
we are given an underlying framework. In *B'reishit*, the universe was
described as "*tohu vavohu*," or chaos. And the Torah begins with
how God pulled out and defined Life itself. The characters in the
Garden of Eden – until Noah – are reactive, and primarily driven by
their own interests, but they are driven: They act in the best interest
of their own lives. Noah enters the picture, and the lesson changes
from self-interest exclusively to concern for God and others around
him. It's with Noah's story that we first understand that we aren't
alone, that we are part of something greater than ourselves. And then
Abraham will come, and he will teach us that we bear responsibility
for all of these elements and must continually strive to do better, to
exceed expectations. The Garden of Eden is the core, like a seed,
with Noah and Abraham additional layers of enlightenment, but
recounting the core reminds us of the purpose of our existence.

And Noah's value in it all? He is the foundation of humanity. At the
very least, we should be good to one another and respectful of the
Creator of the Universe. It's understanding this principle that sets us
on the good path.

---

[1] *Midrash Tanchuma Tazria 5,* as translated and found in Harvey J. Fields,
A Torah Commentary for Our Times Volume One: Genesis (New York:
UAHC Press, 1990), p. 42.

With a Little Help from My Friends

Rabbi Dave Siegel

The story of Noah and his ark is one of the most recognizable sections of the Bible. The story and themes found in the Text are present in all aspects of popular culture, from movies to childrens shows. In these retellings of the story, the writers focus on a few main elements. God decides He is going to destroy the world. Since Noah finds favor with God, He tells him to build an ark in order to save himself, his family, and two members of each species. God floods the world, wiping out all other life and, when the water subsides, Noah and his family leave the ark and rebuild the world. Unfortunately, summaries like this one fail to address one of the most important aspects of the story: Noah's relationship to his community.

The Text states that "Noah was a righteous man" (Gen. 6:9). Given this appellation, one might expect that we would have a record of Noah trying to persuade the people to repent or even have him attempt to persuade God to change His decree. Two of the most powerful moments in the Hebrew Bible are when Abraham tries to prevent God from destroying Sodom and Gomorrah (Gen. 18:20-33) and when Moses convinces God to not destroy the Israelites (Num. 14:11-20). Here the Text is silent regarding Noah's relationship to his community or any attempts he made to save the world around him. This was also something that troubled our rabbis. For instance, there is a midrash where Noah builds the ark over 120 years in the hope that people would ask what he is doing and change their ways when they hear about the impending destruction (Genesis Rabbah 30:7).

Trying to understand Noah's relationship with his community is not simply an academic exercise. I believe this is a key piece to uncovering how this text applies directly to our lives today.

On October 29, 2012, Hurricane Sandy, or as it was more commonly referred to in the media, Superstorm Sandy, swept through the northeastern United States leaving a trail of destruction everywhere that it touched. Although I was living in Queens at the time, many of my family, friends, and students lived on Long Island. Hearing the rain pound against my apartment window and watching the news on television, I could only hope that the people who decided to stay in the flood areas were safe. The news reports described in detail how the water moved in quickly, covering the neighborhoods and trapping many individuals. Unfortunately, some even lost their lives.

Looking at the destruction caused by the water, I could not help but think of *Parsahat Noah*, which we had just read a week and a half earlier. How, upon God's instruction, Noah brought his family and the animals into the ark that he had built and closed the door, knowing that his world would be forever changed. Everyone he knew, the life he knew, would be gone. The Text is silent regarding their reactions when they emerge from the ark. Did the entire world look like the images that we see after natural disasters or in a movie that depicts a post-apocalyptic world? Were there pieces of destroyed homes, remnants of places they used to go, or even the bodies of the animals and individuals that were left behind? What were they thinking, and how did they have the strength to go on? Was there a hint on how these individuals could move forward? Life as they knew it was gone.

In the days following Hurricane Sandy I drove around the neighborhood where I grew up. Houses were destroyed, familiar landmarks were torn from the ground, and the streets were littered with people's treasured possessions. Large dumpsters lined the streets and people, many of whom I'd known my whole life, were throwing out furniture, picture albums, private letters, and toys. Some were even using shovels to lift all of the scattered items. Although Hofstra University made it through the storm relatively unharmed, numerous students and their families were displaced because of severe flooding and physical damage to their homes. Life as they knew it was gone.

Thankfully, unlike Noah, the victims of Hurricane Sandy were not alone. They had their friends, family, and neighbors to support them. People came from local areas, as well as from distant states, to help those affected save what personal items could be salvaged. Lost possessions that were scattered throughout the streets were reunited with their owners, and individuals provided emergency funding where they could. [1] I was particularly proud of the role Hofstra was able to play offering shelter, collecting supplies, providing moral support, and creating the Hofstra University Community Disaster Relief Fund, which assisted full-time Hofstra employees and students who suffered losses.

According to our tradition Hillel taught "Do not separate yourself from the community, and do not trust in yourself until the day of your death." (*Pirkei Avot* 2:5). When we see the rainbow in the sky, it should not serve as a reminder that God will never destroy the world again through water, but as a communal call to action. Through our deeds and ethical behavior, we can control our own destiny, thus insuring there will never be a need to start over again.

---

[1] A special "shout out" to my parents' 12-year old neighbor, Mary Rose, for offering them the allowance she saved, because she wanted to help them so badly.

לֶךְ לְךָ

Lekh Lekha

Born to Run – The Journey

Rabbi David Kalb

One of the greatest songwriters of all time is Bruce Springsteen. I still remember the first time I heard his classic song "Born to Run." It hit me very powerfully with its theme of journey. That is how I feel when I hear the opening of *Lekh Lekha*.

Lekh Lekha tells the story of the rather unusual birth of the Jewish nation. In Genesis 12:1, God commands Abram (who will eventually be known as Abraham): "Go for yourself (*lekh lekha*) from your land, from your relatives, and from your father's house to the land that I will show you." We read no theology, see no miracles, and receive no proof of God's existence. God simply tells Abram to go on a journey. The command itself is also unusual: *lekh lekha*, "Go for yourself." The Torah could have simply used the single word *lekh*, "Go," and identify where Abram was coming from and where he was headed. It is unnecessary to add the word *lekha*, "for yourself." The word *lekha* seems superfluous and somewhat awkward. It is more logical to say, simply, "Go." Why *lekh lekha*? Perhaps because the Torah teaches us that Abram's journey is a journey of self, not simply of geography. God does not just tell Abram to go on a physical journey, but commands Abram to go on a spiritual journey as well. When God says *lekh lekha*, "Go for yourself," God commands Abram to begin a journey to try to understand God.

The entire story of Torah is the story of journey. We see it in the narratives of each generation of the patriarchs and matriarchs. Skipping Isaac for now, let's examine Rebekah. Rebekah is very comparable to Abraham. Her story can be found in Genesis 24-27. She journeys; she leaves her home and family to go to a new place. As a result of her journey, Rebekah is the one who speaks to God directly. She also engineers the journey of the next generation, which brings us to Jacob, Rachel, and Leah. Jacob's story begins in Genesis 25 and goes through the end of the book of Genesis. Jacob is the paradigm for journey in the Torah. He journeys when he runs away from his brother Esau, after stealing Esau's birthright. He journeys again when he runs away from his father-in-law Laban, who tricks him many, many times. Jacob journeys to Egypt where he is reunited with his son Joseph. All of these journeys are physical journeys but can be seen allegorically as spiritual journeys.

The theme of journey hits its crescendo in the Torah with the story of the Exodus from Egypt. It took the Jewish people forty years to travel from Egypt to Israel. This is an extraordinarily long time for even a large group traveling at a slow pace. A geographic journey, certainly, but the experiences that happened on that journey shaped the nature of the Jewish people.

We became the people we are today because of that journey, and the journey continues. It is the journey that creates meaning in Judaism. The journey takes place on a communal level, but it also must occur on an individual level as well. *Lekh lekha*, "Go for yourself." To emphasize this point of *lekha*, "yourself," we can now return to the story of Isaac. Isaac is the only one of our patriarchs who never leaves his home. He journeys neither literally nor metaphorically. There is a sense, when reading Isaac's story, that he has no ability to see beyond himself or his times. Genesis 27:1 describes Isaac with the words "And his eyes dimmed from seeing." It is a strange way of describing the loss of eyesight. It is as if to say that the events that Isaac saw in his life took his vision away. Perhaps the Torah is telling us that Isaac is not physically blind or that he is not just physically blind.

The Torah is really telling us that Isaac lacks vision. Why does he lack vision? Why is he never able to engage in a journey? Genesis 22 tells the story of the attempted sacrifice of Isaac by his father, now called Abraham. In the end, as we know, Abraham does not sacrifice Isaac. However, the experience has a profound effect on Isaac. At the end of the story, Abraham returns from the sacrifice. The Torah says nothing about Isaac's return. The story ends with the idea that on an metaphorical level Isaac remains on the sacrificial altar for the rest of his life. The experience of near-sacrifice stunts Isaac's ability to journey. We see how important it is for every person to engage in his or her own spiritual journey – *lekh lekha*, Go for yourself. Perhaps the story of the attempted sacrifice teaches us that Isaac, rather than participating in his own journey, was limited and enveloped in his father's journey. Ultimately Abraham found his own way, but Isaac never really did.

It is interesting that the Torah does not explain how Abraham comes to God. Different people come to God in different ways, and if the Torah explained how Abraham, the person who brought monotheism to the world, came to God, following generations would conclude that Abraham's way was the only way. However, there is never only one way. Some come to God through logic, others through history, others through nature, and others through life events.

Communities should offer many ways and approaches of looking and thinking about God. Communities that limit ways of understanding God, limit people and worse yet, they attempt to limit God. Limiting approaches to God thwarts our personal journeys. We all must find our own way, travel our own journey.

Lessons from Stars and Dust

Rabbi Meir Mitelman

I n this *parasha*, God tells Abraham that his descendants will be "like the dust of the earth" (Gen. 13:16), and two chapters later, like the stars (Gen. 15:5). In the next *parasha*, Vayeira, the angel who stops Abraham from offering Isaac as a sacrifice says, in God's name,

> ...*Because you have done this and not withheld your son, your favored one, I will bestow my blessing on you and make your descendants as numerous as the stars of heaven and the sands of the seashore...* (Gen. 22:16-17).

One interpretation of the metaphors is obvious: There will be countless numbers of Jewish people. But why is there a need for both metaphors representing how plentiful the Jewish people will be? Does each one represent an idea that the other does not?

According to one midrash, the meaning of comparing the Jewish people to the dust of the earth is that just as dust outlives all those who tread upon it, so God promised Abraham that his offspring would outlive all the nations that would persecute them. The approach of another midrash, focusing on the stars, is that just as no one can conquer the stars, likewise no nation will ever succeed in exterminating Israel.

Rabbi Yosef Dov Soloveitchik (1820-1892), a renowned Talmudic scholar, suggests there are, indeed, two different meanings. One is that when we look up at the sky, we see countless individual stars, each seeming far away from one another. The other metaphor, "like the dust of the earth," reminds us that it is virtually impossible to pick up one infinitesimal piece of dust.

He then continues with an approach to integrating what we see above and below into our lives. When we look up at the sky, we see individual stars, symbolic of the importance of remembering that each of us is unique and has precious, infinite value. When we look at the dust of the earth, we realize we cannot pick up one tiny piece of dust. Only when millions of particles of dust are packed together is there earth to walk on or, to use the metaphor in Genesis 22:17, "sand on the seashore."

We learn from these two different images that even though each of us is unique, like each dazzling star, we are in some ways insignificant if we are not knit together closely as a community with a sense of responsibility for one another.

I would like to suggest a different approach to the meaning of the two analogies. There is a universal aspect to the stars and the dust of the earth. The stars are beacons of light to all human beings throughout the world, and the dust of the earth is the foundation that all people throughout the world walk upon.

The metaphor comparing the Jewish people to stars can teach us that we need to be a source of light, bringing strength, healing, and hope to everyone whose world is dark with loneliness, poverty, illness, and despair.

Similarly, perhaps we can learn from the metaphor comparing us to the dust of the earth that we must partner with God by being solid ground for all people whose lives are battered by life's hardships. How? By providing them with food, clothing, shelter, and even just emotional support.

In *To Heal a Fractured World*, Rabbi Jonathan Sacks, former Chief Rabbi of Great Britain, says,

> As long as there is hunger…and treatable disease in the world, there is work for us to do. As long as nations fight, and men hate, and corruption stalks the corridors of power; as long as there is unemployment and homelessness, depression and despair, our task is not yet done, and we hear, if we listen carefully enough, the voice of G-d asking us, as he asked the first humans, "Where are you?"

May we all be able to answer that question with "Hineni," Here I am.

Journeys of Discovery, Journeys Toward Perfection

Rabbi Daniel Treiser

*P*arashat *Lekh Lekha* represents an important turning point in the Torah. Until this point, the Torah's concern was to introduce the early stories of humanity, from our origins in the Creation story to understanding elements of human nature through the well-known tales of Adam and Eve, Cain and Abel, Noaḥ, and the Tower of Babel. But then the Torah turns its attention to one man and his family, our family.

We don't know much about this one man named Abram. Our *parasha* doesn't begin his story until he is 75 years old, though the midrash has many tales of his younger days. His story begins with a call from God: "Go forth from your land, from your birthplace, from the house of your father, to the land that I will show you. I will make you a great nation, I will bless you. You will be a blessing and I will make your name great" (Gen. 12:1-2).

The command to leave on this journey, from which the *parasha* derives its name, is a grammatically unique construct. Two words, each just two letters long – a *lamed* followed by a final *khaf* – that look identical in written Hebrew. That unique formulation could perhaps mean that God was speaking in the imperative: "Get up! Get going!" Perhaps it is a sign that God intends for Abram to be sure he is the audience: "You! Abram! Go!" The great commentator Rashi explains that the two words imply two different journeys, one for Abraham's enjoyment and one for his own good.

The words can be interpreted in a different way, however, even according to their traditional pronunciation. *Lekh* is a command form of the verb, "Go!" *Lekha*, the second word, represents something more. It can read to be composed of a prefix meaning "to" or "towards" and a suffix meaning the singular masculine "you." Understood that way, the command may instead read, "Go to yourself."

Beginning a journey can be a challenge. Fear of what the future may hold can be immobilizing. The comforts of home and current situations make it easier simply to stay put. So the command tells Abram that he must take this journey. But even more importantly, perhaps God is telling Abram that he must do more than simply go to a new home. This journey will be one of self-discovery. Along the way he will find his hidden potential and the role he is destined to fill. He is to be a patriarch, the founder of a great, blessed nation. But without going on the journey, without getting away from the old, idol-worshipping ways of his neighbors in Haran, he will never discover the truth about himself and all that he could truly become.

The journey that Abram must take is not an easy one. Before his wandering is complete, Abram will face challenges, settle arguments, and go to battle. He will negotiate with kings and bargain with God. But he will also have moments of wonder and visits from angels. He will see his family grow, and he will enter into a covenantal relationship with God, marked by the changing of his name to Abraham.

Near the end of the *parasha*, God gives Abraham the sign of the covenant, instructing him, "...you and your descendants throughout the ages shall keep My covenant. This is the covenant you shall keep between Me and you and all your descendants after you: every male shall be circumcised" (Gen. 17:9-10). From that time until today, circumcision has been one of the hallmark traditions of the Jewish people. Even with the disappearance of so many other Jewish practices, circumcision remains. In times of danger for the Jewish community, enemies would outlaw it, yet Jews would face punishment or even death to keep this tradition alive.

In our modern world there are some who argue that the ritual of *brit milah* should be abolished, for it is an archaic form of barbarism that parents force upon their young children. Since there are medical studies that support both sides of the debate, there is no easy scientific way to settle it. The power of circumcision remains, then, in its power as one of our oldest customs, a vital link to our history, a connection to thousands of years of Jews who have kept this tradition alive, even in our darkest times. And more than that, circumcision continues the lesson from the beginning of the portion. In a midrash, a Roman general challenges the great Rabbi Akiva. The general states that if God was truly powerful and wanted male children circumcised, God would have created them that way already. Akiva replies, "God gave us all the commandments so that we might perfect ourselves by performing them. God wished that we would take on the responsibility of perfecting ourselves and the world through the practice of the commandments. The commandment of circumcision reminds us that, just as we need to improve ourselves physically, so do we need to improve ourselves and our world spiritually."

Rabbi Akiva teaches that circumcision is a reminder that the journey is not yet complete. Our lives are journeys toward perfection, making ourselves and our world better. We have been given the tools and the skills. We've been given the path to improvement through the teachings of our Jewish tradition. *Lekh lekha* reminds us that it is time for us to get moving on that journey, so let's go!

וירא

—

Vayeira

What Do We See?

Loen Amer

Names of *parashiyot* are determined by the first important word of the *parasha*, irrespective of content or theme. *Vayeira*, however, is a *parasha* whose name also relates to its content. *Vayeira* means "and He showed Himself," which comes from the root *yera*, "to see," which is a common thread in the many stories told in these five chapters. Characters in *Vayeira* see, or fail to see, what is apparent and what is revealed in the world around them.

Sitting in his tent at the beginning of *Vayeira*, what did Abraham see? *Vayeira* begins with theophany, God showing Godself to Abraham, but the next verse describes Abraham seeing three men. God showed Godself to Abraham – those three angels – but tradition states that Abraham saw three strangers yet offered them hospitality suitable for divine beings.

Equally hospitable is Lot, who, sitting at the city gate, sees two men and persuades them to be his guests. But the people of Sodom surround his home, demanding, "Bring [the men] out to us, that we may be intimate with them" (Gen. 19:5). While Lot and Abraham welcome defenseless strangers, the people of Sodom see outsiders as victims, whom they can dominate sexually to express their own power with impunity. They are mistaken. These men are not vulnerable; they are powerful emissaries of God, who strike the mob "with blinding light" (Gen.19:11). Having seen the angels as victims, the crowd is left sightless for their last night alive before Sodom and Gomorrah are destroyed.

After giving birth to Isaac, "Sarah saw the son whom Hagar the Egyptian had borne to Abraham" (Gen. 21:9). Concerned that Ishmael will take Isaac's inheritance, Sarah has Hagar and Ishmael sent away. This is not kind. While not violent, as was the mob in Sodom, Sarah acts without hospitality to someone who has been part of her household since birth. She sees Ishmael only as Isaac's antagonist. Has truth been revealed by her motherhood, or is she blinded by paranoia?

Expelled from home, Hagar and Ishmael wander without water, and Hagar believes Ishmael's death is imminent. But they are saved: "God opened her eyes and she saw a well of water" (Gen. 21:19). The well wasn't created; it had always been there, but Hagar's eyes were closed to what was right in front of her. The revelation of life-giving water is a mark of divine favor, suggesting to me that Sarah inaccurately saw Ishmael as Isaac's enemy.

The climax of the *parasha* is the binding of Isaac. God instructs Abraham to offer Isaac, "as a burnt offering on one of the heights that I will point out to you" (Gen. 22:2). They depart, and "on the third day Abraham looked up and saw the place from afar" (Gen. 22:4). How was this place revealed? Did Abraham wait three days, preparing for the terrible deed? Did he find the site quickly, eager to do God's bidding? The place is the last thing seen in the text as the action of the story rises until an angel stops Abraham, just in time. Then, finally, "Abraham looked up, his eye fell upon a ram, caught in the thicket by its horns" (Gen. 22:13). Like Hagar's well, the ram had been there, but Abraham did not see it on his own.

This story is introduced as a test, begging the question: Did Abraham pass? Traditionally he succeeded, pleasing God with his willingness to surrender what he valued most. But after he binds Isaac, God never again speaks directly to Abraham; there is no more theophany. Interactions between God and Abraham are conducted via angels. As someone horrified by Abraham's compliance, who cannot accept his Nuremberg defense of just following God's orders, I interpret this to mean he failed. I want Abraham to be punished for his horrible almost-act, his intimacy with God broken.

"Abraham named that site *Adonai-yireh*," which means "the Lord is seen," giving rise to a proverbial phrase, "On the mount of the Lord there is vision" (Gen. 22:14). While the *parasha* begins with God revealing Godself only to Abraham, the climax of *Vayeira* concludes with more egalitarian access to Revelation. The aphorism suggests that anyone on Moriah can "*yireh*," or experience "vision" there.

We can all see hidden truths, but often fail. Unlike Abraham willingly offering Isaac, we must have the courage to look critically and see what is good. We must welcome like Abraham and Lot, not victimize like the mob at Sodom; we cannot be blinded by fear for the future like Sarah, or fail to see what is in front of us like Hagar and Abraham. To do so, we must be somewhere – morally, emotionally, spiritually – where we have access to that vision of good.

All Are Welcome

Rabbi Fred Greene

Vayeira eilav Adonai b'eilonei Mamre – the Eternal appeared to Abraham in the plains of Mamre, where he made his camp. We read that God appears to Abraham, but when Abraham looks up from the door of his tent, he sees three men who are God's messengers. Thinking that they are mere wanderers, Abraham offers them a morsel of bread but prepares a feast. He has them wash the dust off their feet and makes sure they are comfortable before they carry on with their journey.

In our day, we don't think much about hospitality. If we go to someone else's house, maybe we will bring flowers, chocolates, or some small gift. In Abraham's day, the hospitality of a host could save your life.

Have we become more lax about it because we don't need hospitality in the same way as did our ancestors? We tend to own cars and cell phones, and we subscribe to emergency road services; but a journey through the Judean wilderness posed great risk, and a host provided safety.

The rabbis saw an important lesson in this chapter. We recall Abraham and Sarah's graciousness and hospitality at every Jewish wedding ceremony when we raise the *huppah* (wedding canopy), hoping that the newly married couple will be kind and welcoming to the guests and strangers who come their way.

How much more so should we keep our synagogue doors open to those seeking ways to connect with Judaism, the Jewish community, and God. Many are fortunate to be part of a synagogue community that strives to be there for those who walk through our doors and enter our tents. Our hospitality can also save us from the unknown in the wilderness. Our congregations can provide sanctuary from a complicated, often chaotic world.

But let's be honest: Have synagogues always done their best? Certainly not. Have we grown in countless ways? I believe we have. The last few decades have brought enormous change and growth. But of course, there is more to do.

In the 2014 Pew Study entitled, *A Portrait of Jewish Americans*, we learn a number of things. (Actually, rabbis already knew its findings; it just confirmed what we knew with statistics.) American Jews overwhelmingly say they are proud to be Jewish and have a strong

Jewish identity. But the study tells us that one in five Jews (22%) describe themselves as having no religion. It is something that other faith communities are encountering throughout our country. Americans – not just Jews – are shrinking away from having any formal religious connection. Forty-five percent of "nones" (those who say they have no religion) believe in God, so it is not that they want no religion; they simply are wary of religious institutions.

So what do we do?

We should welcome the stranger in our midst – but this time, the strangers are other Jews! We must make sure that every single Jewish individual (and those who love them) is cared for and supported. We need to think differently as leaders and mean it when we say that all are welcome. We need to be more responsive to the needs of the disenfranchised, disillusioned, and uninspired. Then, those who have written off the one institution that sustains Judaism and the Jewish People will need to take another look. They will need to let go of the notion of being served as consumers and replace it with a perspective of being engaged through relationships. Those who want to perpetuate a Judaism that is compelling need to be willing to be met and to grow together with others in community.

I don't work in a store. I have nothing to sell. As rabbis, my colleagues and I extend our hands to all who want a meaningful connection. We seek to be a part of communities that are vibrant, innovative, and serious. But that also means we need partners.

I believe in these "institutions" – these synagogues; they are our safe places. It is where we learn and teach. It is where we struggle to find God and even, at times, to challenge God. We search for answers, but more often we search for questions.

Our synagogues are like the tent of Abraham and Sarah. We seek to be open, safe, inclusive, accessible, and hospitable. Do we miss the mark sometimes? Sure we do. After all, we are human.

However, we have good people who want to make a difference in the Jewish journeys of others. All are welcome in our tents.

Eyes of the World

Rabbi David Kalb

This week's *parasha* teaches through narrative the mitzvah of *hakhnasat orhim*, the commandment of welcoming guests. At the beginning of the *parasha*, Abraham is found sitting in his *ohel*, which according to the midrash *Yalkut Shmoni* on *Parashat Vayeira*, was designed in such a way that he could see visitors coming from all directions. In essence it was open on all four sides, enabling Abraham not only to see any travelers who might be coming, but also to indicate that those travelers would be welcome to food, drink, or shelter.

Abraham was so committed to being open to welcoming guests that, according to the Talmud in *Bava Metzia* 86b, he sat out in the hot sun despite the fact that this was the third day after his *brit milah*. According to Genesis 17:24, Abraham was 99 years old at the time; imagine the painful state he was in, recovering from his circumcision at such an old age, without the benefit of the anesthesia we have today. The *parasha* goes on to describe in detail how Abraham takes care of three travelers, who according to Rashi (Gen. 18:2) were *melakhim*, angels sent by God. He welcomes them and serves them a meal.

Obviously, this story is about Abraham's willingness to open himself to guests. However, there is a deeper meaning as well. It is a powerful, symbolic idea that Abraham's tent is opened up on all four sides. Perhaps we are supposed to learn through this imagery, and through Abraham himself, a lesson about what it means to be "open."

Mitzvot are not just about fulfilling certain religious responsibilities. Part of their purpose is to transform us. When a mitzvah obligates us to do something kind for another person, there is more to it than just the kind act that we are performing in that moment – that mitzvah should ingrain kindness and compassion as a true, reflexive characteristic within us. Therefore, when we are commanded to be open to welcoming guests, an additional goal is, through that welcoming spirit, to become open people, with open eyes, hearts, minds, and hands.

Open eyes: The first lines of the *parasha* are full of eye imagery and openness imagery. Genesis 18:1: "God appeared to him [Abraham] in the plains of Mamre while he was sitting at the opening of his tent." 18:2: "He lifted his eyes and saw: And behold, three men were standing over him, and he saw, so he ran toward them from the opening of his tent." First God appears to Abraham while he is sitting at the opening of his tent. Then Abraham's eyes see the three guests that he will welcome into his tent. Last, he sees the guests and runs toward them from the opening of his tent. The Torah makes it clear that Abraham was a person with open eyes, eyes which saw divinity operating in the world and detected the needs of other human beings.

Open heart: What gave Abraham the ability to see God? Why was Abraham so open to helping others? His eyes were open because his heart was open; his capacity to see was an extension of his capacity to feel. Abraham's lesson is a fundamental and timeless one: that by opening our hearts to others, we open our own eyes; when we open our own eyes, we see even more deeply the needs of others. The more open we are to seeing others, the more open we are to seeing God. Deuteronomy 15:7: "You shall not harden your heart." On the contrary, you should open your heart.

Open mind: As his open heart is predicated on his open eyes, so his open mind is an extension of his innate openness. Abraham would not be able to see and feel God's presence in the world if his mind was not open to the possibility. He would not be able to be open to the opportunity to help others unless his mind was open and compassionate. What is his lesson to us? No less than we should strive to open our minds. We should open them to people who have different ideas than we do, who have different worldviews, different religious or political views. Job 36:3-4: "I will fetch my knowledge from afar, and will ascribe righteousness to my Maker. For truly my words are not false; one that is upright in mind is with you." How do we become upright in mind? By having an open mind.

Open hand: Finally, Abraham takes the openness of his emotions and perceptions and translates them into action: He opens his hand. How open are our own hands to welcoming others, to helping others? Perhaps this is how we should understand the line in Psalm 145:16: "You open up your hands and satisfy every living thing according to its desire." The line refers to God feeding the hungry. But does God have hands? Yes. We are God's hands. When we feed the poor we are operating as God's open hands.

Open eyes, open hearts, open minds, open hands. During *shaharit*, there is the mitzvah to wear *tefillin*. *Tefillin* are worn between the eyes, on the heart, around the head – which contains the mind – and around the arm and hand. Perhaps part of the message of *tefillin* is that we should look at the world with our open eyes and see the problems that exist in the world. What we see should affect us emotionally – our hearts should be open. Then we need to think with an open mind about what we should do and then, with an open hand, we should do something about it.

Nor is *tefillin* the only mitzvah that uses the open eyes, heart, mind, and hand. When we light Shabbat candles we use open eyes, heart, mind, and hand. When we give *tzedakah* we use open eyes, heart, mind, and hand. When we do *bikur holim* we use open eyes, heart, mind, and hand.

On some level, every mitzvah we perform requires us to open our eyes, hearts, minds, and hands. However we should not only perform mitzvot in this way. We should embody at all times in our life the idea of opening our eyes, hearts, minds, and hands.

The title of this article is from the song, "Eyes of the World" by The Grateful Dead. The Grateful Dead is my favorite band. They are the greatest band in the land. "Eyes of the World" is a song that I have always loved, and I think it relates a little to this article. Therefore, I would like to conclude by sharing the chorus of the song.

Wake up to find out that you are the eyes of the world.
But the heart has its beaches its homeland and thoughts of its own.
Wake now; discover that you are the song that the morning brings.
But the heart has its seasons its evenings and songs of its own.

חיי שרה

Ḥayyei Sarah

To Life!

Rabbi Noam Raucher

My grandmother recently passed away. I realize that is a heavy opening statement to make for a *d'var Torah*. But, as to be expected, it is hard to think about many other things in the shadow of death. I have plenty of distractions, yet my attention is always drawn back to my grandmother...

My family asked that I perform the funeral for her. As the only rabbi in the family, it was a duty and an honor to provide the service. So I took a breath and did my best. The funny thing is that in the biting winter air, among the two-and-a-half feet of snow on the ground at Montefiore Cemetery, while tears were freezing to my family's faces, I could not cry. I could only smile.

Do not get me wrong; I miss my grandmother very much. When she passed she was 93 years old. Even if the last few years were not as great as they could have been, that is a long time to be alive! I had the privilege of knowing her for 35 of those years.

I remember her as a tall and elegant woman. Like a solider in some ways. She seemed to yearn for the finer things in life. She kept a very tidy home and presented herself the same way. She was always patient and calm, and she never really seemed to get in a fuss over childish antics. When needed, she had a loving sarcasm which taught you a lesson and made you laugh at the same time.

With all these memories I have swirling around in my head, I do not really think about my grandmother's death at all. Rather, all I seem to do is think about her life.

The Torah asks of us the same thing as we read this *parasha, Ḥayyei Sarah* – Sarah's Life. In telling us about Sarah's death, it opens by telling us that she lived. When it points us to her life we have no other choice but to recall her story: How she was daring and brave for her husband (Gen.12:11-13), how she grew and found blessings and God in her life (Gen. 17:15-16), how she cared for guests in her home (Gen. 18:6), how she even surprised herself in her old age by sustaining the birth of a child (Gen. 18:9-12), and how, finally becoming a mother, she found motherhood challenging (Gen. 21:2-10).

Not only did she live, but did so for 127 years! With all this history it is nearly impossible to think of Sarah as dead at all – just as it is with my grandmother.

We may miss the matriarchs of our biblical and our present days. And it is hard to let go of someone who has been a fixture in our own lives for so long. They appear, in some ways, like a missing piece of a not-quite-completed puzzle. Just the outline remains.

But our biggest mistake would be to think that the only thing that exists is the outline, as if to say that our loved ones are defined solely by their deaths. No, that can't be. Not for us and certainly not for them. The Torah recognizes Sarah's life in the face of her death as a way of saying people are defined by the lives they lead, not by passing from our world to the next. We may mourn them in their absence, but we live our lives in celebration of the lives they lived.

In our tradition, when someone dies, we comfort the bereaved by saying *Zikhrono l'vrakha* (for a man) / *Zikhronah l'vrakha* (for a woman) – "May their memory be a blessing." It is the memory of their lives that is a tangible blessing in our own when we think about the indelible mark they have left on us. In that way we sanctify the lives they lived and carry them with us every day forward.

Abraham's Model of Ethical Ownership

Micah Guerin Weiss

The opening of *Parashat Ḥayyei Sarah* finds Abraham in Hebron, mourning the death of Sarah, and trying to buy a plot of land where he can bury his beloved wife. The entire first chapter of the *parasha* is devoted to the detailed choreography of Abraham negotiating with *b'nei ḥeit* (the inhabitants of Hebron) to buy the place he has set his sights on: the Cave of Machpelah. This exchange gives us a special window into Abraham's ethical conduct while engaging with a large group of people.

One of the first things I notice in the exchange is how humble Abraham is in his speech and manner. Word has spread throughout the land that God has taken a special liking to Abraham. He has amassed great wealth, has a stellar reputation, and by all indications Abraham is a big man about town. It is fitting then that *b'nei ḥeit* greet Abraham with a great deal of respect:

> Hear us, my lord: you are the elect of God among us. Bury your dead in the choicest of our burial places; none of us will with-hold his burial place from you for burying your dead (Gen. 23:6).

Abraham understandably could accept the people's offer at face value and grab the Cave of Machpelah. After all, didn't God promise this land to his descendants? Ephron the Hittite, the owner of the cave, even offered to give it to Abraham for free:

> No, my lord, hear me: I give you the field and I give you the cave that is in it; I give it to you in the presence of my people. Bury your dead. (Gen. 23:11).

But Abraham does a curious thing; he makes a huge point of prostrating and humbling himself before the people. In verse 4, Abraham introduces himself by saying, "I am a stranger and sojourner with you," and then, in verse 7, we learn that "Abraham rose and bowed low to the people of the land, to the Hittites." In verse 12, Abraham bows yet again: "And Abraham bowed low before the people of the land." Abraham eventually accepts the price Ephron offers for the land – 400 shekalim – without an argument, a price which classically is understood to be exorbitantly high.

So what are we to make of all this? The *Midrash HaGadol* notices Abraham's demeanor and offers a beautiful analysis of his behavior:

> *Come and see the humility of Abraham our father! The Holy One blessed be He promised to give him and his seed the land forever. Yet now he could only find a burial ground by paying a high price, and yet he did not question the attributes of the Holy One blessed be He and did not complain. Moreover, he addressed the inhabitants of the land with humility, as it is said, "I am a stranger and a sojourner with you." Said the Holy One blessed be He to him , "You humbled yourself; by your life I shall make you a Lord and a prince over them."*

In the understanding of this midrash, even though Abraham was endowed with great privilege through God's blessing, he doesn't let it go to his head and become entitled and self-centered. By the midrash's interpretation, you can even say it is precisely Abraham's display of humility and respect, not his power and wealth, that inspire *b'nei ḥeit* to address him as, "my lord, you are the elect of God among us."

The Chizkuni, a 13th-century French commentator on the *Humash*, picks up on this same point by asking a question about a repetition of the verse, "And Abraham rose and bowed down to the people of the land, to *b'nei ḥeit*." The Chizkuni asks,

> *If Abraham is buying this plot of land from Ephron, why does he bow down to the people of the land and b'nei ḥeit? And why does he do it twice? Abraham needed all of them. Though Ephron had sold him the field, Abraham was not authorized to use it as a burial ground without the permission of his fellow citizens. He therefore had to rise up in order to bow down to all of them, even to those behind him...*

In this reading, not only does Abraham respectfully show humility before *b'nei ḥeit*, who then possessed the land of Hebron, but to the common folk of the town as well. Abraham understands the complicated dynamics of coming into a new neighborhood as an outsider and the importance of establishing communal buy-in with the folks with whom you will be sharing space.

Abraham's interactions with Ephron and *b'nei ḥeit* remind me of my own experiences moving into a new apartment a few years ago, when I moved to Crown Heights, Brooklyn, one of the fastest gentrifying neighborhoods in New York City. All I had to do in order to move in was sign a lease and drag my stuff up the stairs. But just because

I "own" my apartment by having signed a lease doesn't mean that I am ethically entitled to live there. Landlords are looking for folks just like me to pay the huge rent increases they're charging, but the long-term residents in my building don't benefit at all. These residents feel as if they are not being shown respect.

In trying to follow the ethical model of Abraham, I've taken the time to meet each of my neighbors and learn their stories. I've joined the community block association, created an online news alert to stay up to speed on the neighborhood happenings, and changed my voter registration to vote locally. I've joined a synagogue in the neighborhood, and I volunteer at an anti-violence center working to reduce gun violence in Crown Heights. I respect the people who have already worked hard to create a community.

No one told Abraham he had to treat the people of Hebron with respect, but he did and God expected it. There is no one "correct" way to be caught up in the politics of gentrification, but we should be expected to find ways to be the most responsible and respectful neighbors we can be. How much more wonderful it is when people are truly happy offering you the things you need. How much better a foundation to live in peace.

Avodah

(Love is…Hard Work.)

Rabbi Rachel Wiesenberg

"Rebekah raised her eyes and she saw Isaac. She fell from atop the camel."

"Isaac then brought her into the tent of his mother Sarah, and he took Rebekah as a wife. Isaac loved her, and thus found comfort after his mother's death."

> I do not believe in love
> at first sight.
> I don't.
> Really.
> BUT…

One morning during my junior year at Hofstra, I walked into the Axinn Library and laid eyes on Jonathan Wiesenberg. Immediately, I felt something. Electricity? Butterflies? Lust? A call from *Hashem* that my *beshert* stood before me?

I know in the movie, *Bambi*, it's called being "twitterpated." To use the imagery from *Hayyei Sarah*, I got knocked right off my camel.

My point is, there was a connection. This connection would eventually turn into Love, but it was not love for a long time. Love takes work. Hard Work.

Rebekah and Isaac would agree with me. When Rebekah first sees Isaac, she feels "twitterpated," but she does not feel love. Isaac takes Rebekah as his wife, and *then* he loves her.

Wait, what? I thought "First comes love, then comes marriage"? Not really.

Ramban understands this. He teaches that Isaac's love for his wife stems from her righteousness and good deeds. That kind of observation can only come with time. Chizkuni goes a (slightly Oedipal) step further, teaching that Rebekah's righteous deeds reminded Isaac of his mother, and therefore he loved her. Whether it is from Ramban, Chizkuni, or just your own *peshat* reading, it seems pretty clear, especially when you take the rest of their long marriage into account, that Rebekah and Isaac have to do the Work of Love before they can Feel Love.

Love *is* Hard Work. Relationships take time and energy.

How much the more so if you want a relationship with God.

I am lucky, I know, to feel God's presence in my life. Not all day every day, but I do feel it. I have felt it. Some people do not have a relationship with God because there is suffering in their lives – illness, loss, pain of some kind or another. Those human beings need comfort from their loved ones. They are not in a healthy mindset to do the Work, most often, of being in a relationship with God.

Some of these people are, understandably, angry with God...but that is still a relationship. When I am angry with Jon (he knows, because I call him Jonathan) or when he is angry with me, we know that those are actually some of the growing pains that must occur for a deep, meaningful bond to emerge. Anger does not break a bond with God. Apathy does. Silence does.

I am not talking about people who are going through a crisis. There are other Jews out there who simply don't feel like meeting God half way.

Relationships, as the word denotes, involves relating to someone or, in God's case, some thing. As Martin Buber writes over and over again, "relation is reciprocity," relationships are based on give-and-take. As Jews desiring a relationship with God, that give-and-take can come in many forms.

Tefillah.
Tzedekah.
Tikkun olam.
Halakha.

When you are a Jew, you have to *do something*. You have to put in the effort of making this relationship work. You can't just show up on the High Holidays and wonder why you haven't heard from God all year long. Did you "pick up the phone" yourself?

Buber felt "...in truth, there is no God-seeking because there is nothing where one could not find Him." I do not agree 100% with Buber, but I do believe that as Jews, we must pray, study, act, and renew for God. With God. To God. If you do not pray or study or make the world a better place, when do you expect to feel God in your life?

If my husband only acts like my partner on our anniversary, we do not have much of a marriage. It is the other 364 days of the year when the real Work of our relationship is done. It is the same with

God. We cannot expect God to "show up" for us if we do not "show up" for God. Or, as Buber beautifully writes:

> That you need God more than anything, you know at all times in your heart. But don't you know also that God needs you – in the fullness of His eternity, you? How would man exist if God did not need him, and how would you exist? You need God in order to be, and God needs you…"

תולדת

—

Tol'dot

How Do We View Death; How Do We View Life?

Bob Margulies

In the *parasha* of *Tol'dot*, there is one particular episode that gives a meaningful perspective on life and death. The *parasha* begins with the birth of twins to Rebekah: Jacob and Esau, two boys who, while in the womb, are described as already being diametrically different from each other. Among the first encounters described (Gen. 25:29-34) is the sale by Esau of his birthright to Jacob. The encounter begins as Jacob is making lentil soup. Esau comes in from the field, says he is hungry and wants the soup. Jacob says, "Sell me your birthright," which Esau agrees to and sells it for a pot of soup. During this sale, Esau specifically states, "I am going to die, so what advantage will my birthright do for me?" After the sale, and after Esau eats the lentil soup, he leaves; the Torah notes that "Esau despised the birthright."

What is noteworthy about the sale of the birthright is that according to one of most famous biblical commentaries, Rashi, it took place on the day of Abraham's death. Abraham was the grandfather of Jacob and Esau. Rashi explains that Jacob was making lentil soup to comfort his father Isaac, who was mourning the loss of his father. Lentils are served to the mourners because they are round and thus symbolize the circular nature of life. In addition, when the Torah mentions that Esau was out in the field, a midrash notes that Esau had been out hunting and that he had committed various cardinal sins that day. The very day that Esau engages in certain amoral activities is the day he sells the birthright.

A deeper view of the sale of the birthright suggests that when Jacob and Esau negotiate the sale of the birthright, they really are demonstrating their individual perspectives on life and death. It is suggested that the different activities in which Jacob and Esau involved themselves on this day reflect their two diametrically opposed responses to the death of Abraham. We can easily imagine how Abraham's death evoked not only personal grief for his family and close peers but also serious questions of faith. There were likely many people who wondered how a righteous man of Abraham's stature, with whom God formed a special, eternal bond, and who was chosen as founder of God's treasured nation, was deserving of death. If human mortality always seems cruel and troubling, the inevitable death of the righteous – particularly a man with whom God made a formal covenant – is especially difficult to accept. Jacob responded to this unfathomable tragedy by preparing lentils, by contemplating the reality of certain fixed, immutable rules of nature which elude human comprehension and certain questions that cannot be answered. Jacob's lentil soup thus signifies his somber acceptance of the inscrutable notion of human mortality, his recognition that we do not and cannot have answers to questions such as Abraham's death, and must instead lower our heads and humbly submit to the divine will.

Esau reacted in the precise opposite manner, rejecting the entire system of monotheistic belief. If Abraham could die, Esau assumed there is no purpose to living a noble, disciplined, spiritual life. This explains Esau's response to Jacob's offer of soup in exchange for the birthright: "Look, I am going to die; why do I need the birthright?" In response to Abraham's death, Esau despaired from finding meaning in his life. Whereas Jacob responded with lentils, with somber reflection and deepening his commitment to living a life of ideals, Esau decided to commit his life to vanity, denying the existence of any deeper layers of meaning beneath the superficial layer of the vain pleasures of the world. This superficial perspective is perhaps expressed by his description of Jacob's lentils as *ha-adom ha-adom ha-zeh*, "this red stuff" (Gen. 25:30). Esau did not bother to identify the essence of the food simmering on the stove. He limited his vision to the external physical appearance, much as he had limited his perspective on life to the superficial level of physical indulgence.

Jacob and Esau's different reactions to the death of Abraham thus represent different responses to the inexplicable tragedies that plague humanity. Jacob responds with humble submission, accepting the limits of human understanding and recognizing the value, meaning, and purposefulness of life despite the harsh realities of the world. Esau, by contrast, sees only the absurdities of the world, without searching for the deeper layers of meaning and purpose.

If we were just physical bodies without souls, then all the physical pleasures of this world would satisfy us. But as human beings with souls – with a *neshama* – we need spiritual nourishment separate and apart from physical nourishment. A person who is focused solely on the physical world is setting himself up for a life of emptiness.

Judaism does not demand that we give up the physical pleasures of this world, but rather that we harness them within the context of our value system. We must dedicate ourselves to the deeper meaning of life, to fulfilling the mitzvot and connecting to the eternal values that God has given us in His Torah and Jewish tradition. We must remember that our souls are on a journey. We spend some time in this world and then go on to an eternal world. With a proper perspective on life we truly can be satisfied, with a deep inner peace that comes from doing the right thing and living in accordance with the teachings and will of God.

––––––––––––

With gratitude to my dear friend, Larry Siegel, who assisted with some of the thoughts herein.

Who Are You?

Rabbi Michael Paley

*P*arashat *Tol'dot* is one of the most thrilling and politically complex narratives in the Torah. Most of the elements that we still cope with in modern Jewish life, both in the international scene and with our Jewish identity, are present in this compact and consequential story. In this *parasha* we find good guys and bad guys, hunters and poets, schemers and tricksters, and we are never told which one is which.

The text opens with a story of a barren wife who finally conceives a child. This is the potent start to the story of Jacob and Esau. Rebekah asks the meaning of all this suffering and she receives an enigmatic answer from the Divine. Genesis 25:23 tells us, "Two nations are in your womb, two separate peoples shall emerge from your body; One people mightier than the other, and the older one shall serve the younger." Rebekah realizes that she has a major decision to make.

The main issue of this *parasha* is which brother will be chosen to continue the special lineage and what blessing will carry him forward. Even though Rebekah already knows which son will be chosen, there is still plenty of improbable drama. Her children are completely different. Esau, a hunter, an outdoor man, hairy and red, just the kind of kid I was afraid of growing up. And Jacob, smooth, a bit alternative, brainy and a stay-at-home boy (Gen. 25:27). The most perplexing question is why not both brothers? After all, they are twins and should be able to collaborate no matter how different they are. From the time of Abraham this has been a question. Why not both Ishmael and Isaac? Why not Jacob and Esau? The more subtle question is, does Rebekah tell Jacob who will win and if not, why not? If she does, why does Isaac act as if Esau has a chance? Is he working out his relationship with Ishmael through his kids? And finally, while God decides to choose Abraham and Isaac, why does Isaac think he can choose Esau to establish the people on his own?

The story of interaction between the brothers captures the intense emotions. Esau is hunting and comes back famished (Gen. 25:29). Jacob is cooking the lentils and, armed only with their aroma, he Is able to outsmart Esau for the birthright. Now we turn to the main event and the resolution of these questions. Isaac is old and turns to his son Esau with the same words that he heard going up the mountain with his father to be sacrificed; he says to Esau, "*B'ni*, My son" (like Gen. 22:8) and Esau responds, "*Hineni*, Here I am." Isaac tells

Esau to hunt and then prepare a dish for him, but Rebekah overhears the request and intervenes on behalf of her younger but chosen son. "Esau is hairy and I am smooth skinned" Jacob says (Gen. 27:11). Rebekah dresses Jacob in Esau's clothes and covers his arms with skins. When Isaac asks Jacob which son he is, Jacob replies, "I am Esau, your first born...give me your innermost blessing, the blessing of your soul" (Gen. 27:19). Did Isaac know it was Jacob? We know Isaac to be a great prophet, but even a simple man knows his sons by more than sight. Rebekah must have told Isaac of the oracle of who would establish the nation and the land.

So why cast Jacob as the trickster? We hold much of the legacy of Jacob, the smooth man who uses tricks to come out on top, the one who sees the bigger picture. But there is a deeper meaning here. Jacob says, "I am Esau." Why? At the base level there will be times that we will need to be Esau, the strong one in the physical realm and not simply the spiritual son. But when we do that we must know that we carry both Jacob and Esau within us. We have to know both blessings that Isaac gave that night, the one that says, "Be master over your brothers and let your mother's sons bow to you" (Gen. 27:29), but also the blessing that Esau receives which says, "Yet by the sword you shall live and you shall serve your brother; But when you grow restive, you shall break his yoke from your neck" (Gen. 27:40). Jacob needs to say, "I am Esau" because he must empathize with him and recognize how inseparable he is from his brother and his brother's needs. Isaac's task is to make Jacob know this deeply enough so that we know it today. Of course Isaac knew it was Jacob and understood what Rebekah had to do because of the oracle. To possess the land we must see both Jacob and Esau in ourselves and have compassion for both sides, and only then can we inherit the blessing and the birthright.

Twin Brothers, Twin Urges

Rabbi Daniel Treiser

*P*arashat Tol'dot (Gen. 25:19-28:9) turns the story of our patriarchs on its ear, making the unexpected the expected. From the very beginning, the characters learn that things are not to be as one would assume. After Isaac pleads with God on behalf of his wife Rebekah, she becomes pregnant with twins. The pregnancy does not go smoothly, as the babies wrestle within her. As she seeks answers, God tells Rebekah, "Two nations are in your womb, two peoples shall issue from your body; One shall be mightier than the other, and the older shall serve the younger" (Gen. 25:23). This prophetic message became a driving principle for all that occurs in the *parasha*.

The twins wrestle even as they are born, with the young baby Jacob grabbing the heel of his older brother Esau as they emerge from the womb. As they grow, Esau the hunter spurns his right of primogeniture, selling his birthright to Jacob for a bowl of lentils. Rebekah, knowing the prophecy she received, aids Jacob in deceiving Isaac to receive the blessing of the first-born child. An enraged Esau threatens his brother's life, so Rebekah insists that Jacob flee. She tells Isaac that the local Hittite women bother her (knowing that Esau had already married two Hittite women), so Isaac sends Jacob off to Canaan, Rebekah's homeland, to find a wife. Esau overhears this and decides to marry one of his own cousins among the Ishmaelites.

The image of these two brothers could not be more different. Esau, the outdoorsman, seems to be a man who lives by his urges and appetites. Whatever Esau wants, he takes. He seeks instant gratification. When he comes home from the field famished, he trades all the privileges and rights, the inheritance and future leadership that came with the birthright, just for a bowl of lentil soup Jacob was making. Rashi (commenting on Gen. 25:30) compares him to a camel that stuffs his face. Guided by his immediate urges he marries two Hittite women, much to the dismay of his parents. He lets his sexual appetite overrule his loyalty to family, his commitment to the traditions of his father.

The portrait of Jacob, however, is a very different one. Torah describes him as *tam*, simple, complete, or whole. Jacob prefers to stay close to home, spending time in the tents, and becomes much closer with his mother Rebekah. Throughout Jewish tradition he is described as someone with an eye for the future, someone who has a vision.

He recognizes the importance of inheriting God's covenant from his father Isaac. So when he sees the opportunity to overcome his lower status as the second born, he convinces Esau to trade him the birthright.

The difference between these twins is apparent right from the start. One lives by his urges, acting on his appetites and immediate needs. One is guided by vision, by a plan for future greatness and ultimately a greater good.

This lesson from the Torah is not really so distant from us and our lives. Each of us has a little bit of both Esau and Jacob within us. There are times when we give in to our own urges, and there are times when we delay our own instant gratification for a long-term gain. Do we indulge ourselves in food or alcohol, choosing the immediate pleasure, or do we restrain ourselves, eating in moderation, striving for a healthier lifestyle? Do we spend our money on luxuries, wasting our wealth on the bigger, the better, the flashier things that we don't really need, or do we save our wealth, planning for the future and putting it to good use through charitable donations or support of important community organizations? Do we let our emotions and our egos get the better of us, acting in anger and arrogance, hurting those around us, or do we temper our own feelings, holding back the hurtful words, sparing a loved one or acquaintance the pain those words might cause?

We understand these conflicted drives in Judaism as a struggle. The desire to fulfill our urges, our baser appetites, is associated with the *yetzer hara*, sometimes called the evil inclination. The drive to do the right thing, to forgo those appetites even when they call to us, is called the *yetzer tov*, the good inclination. We have both these drives within us, and life is a struggle between the *yetzer hara* and the *yetzer tov*. Every choice we make is guided by these inclinations.

This is one of the lessons this *parasha* teaches. Neither Jacob nor Esau is perfect. Neither are we. Each of the twins represents a different side of our lives, the urges that cause us to act. If we understand those drives – the reasons we make the choices we do make – then we can better understand their impact as well.

ויצא

Vayeitzei

Love and Marriage...Oy!

Rabbi Scott Aaron

I am not one to get sentimental about days gone by, and I am definitely not one of those rabbis who fervently pray that God return the Jewish community to our way of life *yameinu k'kedem*, which roughly translates from medieval Hebrew to "back in the day." But I do think our Jewish world today would be richer with a little more Yiddish in it. Yiddish is a dialect of German that draws heavily on Hebrew terminology and even uses Hebrew letters as its own alphabet in its written form. Up until the 20th century, European Jews spoke it as their *mama loschen*, mother tongue. Hebrew was used only for sacred things such as prayer and Torah study; Yiddish was the language of the everyday. Assimilation and the growth of modern Hebrew has left few active Yiddish speakers in the Jewish world, but some things still just sound more honest when they are expressed in Yiddish. For instance, take the word *oy*. It translates as "oh" and expresses dismay. When you hear that your mom invited your ex over for dinner just because she misses her, no word expresses your initial reaction like "*oy!*"

Another Yiddish word that really says a lot at once is *nebach*. You use it when you want to describe someone or a situation that is pitiable or unfortunate or just plain unlucky. A related word is *nebbish,* which is a person who embodies the properties of *nebach*, and it really is the perfect word to describe our foremother Leah. Leah was the sister of Rachel, and they were both the wives of Jacob; our tradition says that all of the Jewish people today descended from them. However, while they were both sisters to each other and wives to the same man, they were not equals. Jacob and Rachel's marriage comprises one of the greatest love stories in history, while Jacob and Leah's marriage makes for one of the most tragic stories of unrequited love.

The Torah tells us that Isaac made Jacob promise to not marry a local girl but rather one from his mother's home town, Haran. So Jacob goes there and makes his first stop at the local watering hole in town. Long story short, Jacob buys his first cousin Rachel (and her sheep) a drink, they kiss, and boom goes the dynamite. Rachel's father and Jacob's maternal uncle, Laban, welcomes him to his home and offers Jacob a job as a shepherd. Jacob says he will work for free if he can marry Rachel, and Laban – a real *gonif* (Yiddish for "thief") – agrees that Jacob should work for him for seven years before he can marry her. Jacob agrees and, seven years later, is brought his bride to the honeymoon tent by Laban. Now this being biblical times, there is no mood lighting in the tent so Jacob cannot exactly see Leah, but on your honeymoon you can pretty much get by relying primarily on the sense of touch. However, when the morning sun brightens things up, Jacob rolls over and discovers he is not married to Rachel, who was "of beautiful form and fair to look upon," but to her sister Leah, the one whose "eyes were weak"! It seems Laban pulled a fast one on Jacob and gave him the *nebbish* sister with the nice personality instead. When Jacob complains, Laban agrees to the original plan but only if Jacob works for him another seven years. Jacob loves Rachel so much that he agrees rather than be content with Leah. *Oy, nebach*!

Genesis 29 tells us that God compensates Jacob for his lack of love for Leah by giving her sons, while Rachel remains barren. Childbearing, especially sons, was the mark of a wife's domestic value in biblical times, so Leah hopes to win Jacob's love through her worth rather than her lack of beauty. She bears him four sons, and the Torah tells us after the birth of each one she prays that now Jacob will finally love her. Sadly, rather than feeling *rachmones* (Yiddish for "compassion") for her sister's situation, the Torah tells us Rachel is envious of her instead. So Rachel gives Jacob her servant, Bilhah, in her place in a biblical form of surrogate parenting; Bilhah then has two sons by Jacob. Leah, incensed that her one advantage over Rachel in this marital tug-of-war is being thwarted, gives Jacob her servant, Zilpah, who also gives him two more sons. Leah then bears Jacob another three sons and a daughter herself! The score in this birth battle for Jacob's love is now Leah/Zilpah 10 – Rachel/Bilhah 2, but Rachel will go on to be blessed by God to conceive and bear two more sons for Jacob, including Joseph, whom the Torah describes as Jacob's favorite child. So no matter how hard Leah tried, and she bore him seven sons on her own which is pretty much the definition of the ideal biblical wife, Jacob still gave all of his love to Rachel and withheld his love from Leah. *Oy, nebach* indeed.

Our Sages historically have explained this harsh text as being emblematic of God's hidden knowledge about the future and that the relationship between the sisters was more loving than it seems. However, it is hard to read this text and not see an inherent sense of *umet* (Yiddish for "sadness") for how Jacob treated Leah, the sisters treated each other, and Laban treated all three of them. It seems to embody the Yiddish saying a *tropn libe brengt a mol a yam trern* ("a drop of love can bring an ocean of tears"). However, in our modern time of choosing our own life partners and recognizing that real love can take many different and even unconventional forms, we can be reassured that Yiddish has another saying that recognizes and acknowledges our Jewish lives: *Itlekhs tepl gefint zikh zayn dekl* ("Every pot finds its own lid")!

Raising the Bar

Rabbi Dr. Ronald L. Androphy

Every year, on New Year's Eve and New Year's Day, WQXR, New York's classical music station, plays the one hundred favorite symphonies, concertos, operas, and other works, as voted on by the station's listeners. Almost every year, Antonin Dvorak's Ninth Symphony, *From the New World*, appears among the top ten works. Dvorak, a Czech composer, wrote the symphony after spending several years in the United States. The second, or *Largo*, movement probably takes its form from the spiritual, "Going Home."

"Going Home" can also serve as the title of the second half of *Parashat Vayeitzei* and would refer to our patriarch Jacob's desire to return to Canaan, his home, after spending twenty years in the home of his uncle (and later father-in-law), Laban. Jacob had fled to his uncle's household after fleeing from his brother, Esau. He had served Laban for seven years in order to marry his cousin, Rachel, and, after Laban had deceived him by substituting Leah for her younger sister, Jacob had to slave away for Laban an additional seven years. During this time, Jacob had fathered eleven sons and one daughter.

At this point Jacob expresses a desire to return home, but Laban convinces Jacob to remain in his household. After working for his uncle/father-in-law another six years, Jacob has had enough. He wants to go home. Why? The Torah tells us: First, he hears that Laban's sons (Jacob's brothers-in-law) are slandering him. Second, and most important, "Jacob saw that Laban's manner toward him was not as it had been in the past" (Gen. 31:2). In other words, Jacob perceives that his uncle/father-in-law's attitude towards him has changed.

Many of the commentators have a problem with this. They ask: What is so different about Laban? After all, he is still the same scoundrel he has always been! How is his treatment of Jacob any different than it had been? He is still treating Jacob with the same deceit with which he has been treating Jacob for the past twenty years! What is so different now that compels Jacob to maintain that he must be "Going Home"?

The late, saintly, Rabbi Avraham Yitzchak Kook, the first Chief Rabbi of Palestine, offered a very interesting interpretation of the verse quoted above, in answer to the question: Why does Jacob realize now that he must be "Going Home" immediately? Rabbi Kook suggests that the reason Jacob chose this moment to leave Laban's household is that Jacob saw all of Laban's deceptive conduct, and Jacob realized that Laban's duplicity didn't bother him (Jacob) anymore. Jacob perceived that he had become so accustomed, so inured, so jaded, so desensitized to Laban's lies that he – Jacob – was no longer upset by Laban's evil and vicious conduct. And that frightened Jacob. Laban was still the same devious character he had always been, but it was Jacob who had changed.

No longer was Jacob disturbed by Laban's unethical antics. Jacob realized that, in a sense, he was becoming spiritually polluted by Laban's immorality. And so Jacob understood that since Laban wasn't going to change, he – Jacob – had to flee and return home, lest he become increasingly like Laban. Jacob comprehended that if he were to save his own conscience, his own morals, his own ethical standards, his own personal integrity, he had to flee fast and be "Going Home." Jacob now knew that for the sake of his own moral and spiritual well-being – and for the sake of his young children – he had to be "Going Home."

Rabbi Kook, in his explanation of Jacob's desire to be "Going Home," offers us tremendous insight into our own situation. Haven't we, in several ways, become like Jacob – almost jaded and desensitized to wrongdoing?

Consider the issue of gun violence. Every night (except Shabbat, of course!) I watch the 11:00 news. Almost inevitably the first several news stories involve some act of violence committed by people with illegal guns. How many people must be murdered before society finally reacts? How many lives must be sacrificed before our society realizes that we must limit the ownership and easy availability of guns? But we have become jaded to gun violence, and so we allow guns to proliferate, and with that proliferation comes more and more lives snuffed out by gunshots. (I write this still affected by a tragic and heinous assault on an AME Church in Charleston, SC, in June 2015. This assault resulted in the deaths of nine innocent people – lives taken by a murderer with a gun.)

Or consider the issue of computer hacking. How many people have been victimized by identity theft and, as a result, have lost thousands of dollars and their sterling credit ratings and reputations? But we have become desensitized to the issue. Too many retail outlets, insurance companies, and even the federal government have failed to protect our data. We bury our heads in the sand, like Jacob almost did in regard to Laban's duplicity; we get upset only when identity theft affects us personally.

The same is true concerning Jewish issues. Intermarriage has become so widespread – perhaps affecting as many as 40%-50% of all marriages involving Jews – that we have become desensitized to intermarriage. We shrug our shoulders, utter platitudes like "at least he/she is a nice person," and continue on our way. We no longer express the same level of concern and opposition that we once did. And so intermarriage continues to grow, threatening the survival of the Jewish people and our religion.

And, it seems to me, this same lack of sensitivity applies to many more aspects of life. We have been jaded so by mediocrity – in education (secular and religious), in the service we give and receive, in the products we manufacture and purchase, in the work we perform – that we fail to pursue the quest for excellence which once characterized our nation and our people.

But unlike Jacob, we do not have the option of "Going Home." We are home. This – our society, our community, our home, our workplace, our school, our *shul* – is our home. And, therefore, we must change our home for the better. We must make it a place that reflects the lofty values by which we should live. Our society, our community, our home, our workplace, our school, and our *shul* must be places where we do not allow our consciences, standards, and values to be overwhelmed by complacency and mediocrity. We must strive to raise the bar – to lift the standards, to pursue the ideal – in our quest to create the kind of world that will uplift the human spirit, and the type of Jewish environment that will foster greater Jewish identity, commitment, and observance.

Awakening to the Divine Presence

Rabbi Daniel Treiser

*P*arashat *Vayeitzei* turns the focus of the Torah on the life of our patriarch, Jacob. His story occupies almost the entire latter half of Genesis because he plays such an important role in Jewish tradition, perhaps even the most important. We rightfully hold Abraham in high esteem as the first patriarch, the one who first heard the call from God to go on a journey and become a great nation, thus introducing the idea of monotheism to the world. Yet we do not call ourselves the Children of Abraham. Isaac, the second patriarch, was the literal fulfillment of God's blessing: the son born to Sarah and Abraham when they were 90 and 100 years old respectively, and he was almost sacrificed by his father. Yet we are not called the Children of Isaac. No, instead, Jewish people all around the world are called *B'nai Yisrael*, the Children of Israel, the Children of Jacob.

But why Jacob? This *parasha* raises the question and begins to give us the answer as well. Of the three patriarchs, at first Jacob seems the least likely person to emulate. When we first meet Jacob in Genesis Chapter 25, he seems manipulative, tricking his brother Esau into forgoing his birthright. Jacob then conspires with his mother Rebekah to deceive Isaac and receive the blessing intended for Esau. In *Vayeitzei*, we see a young man with a huge dose of chutzpah, negotiating with his uncle Laban and even bargaining with God to ensure God's protection on his journey.

So again, why Jacob? I think it is because of the process that Jacob models with the very first words of this Torah portion: "Jacob went out from Beersheva" (Gen. 28:10). He left. He learned the lesson of his grandfather Abraham's journey and departed his family's home in Beersheva. Jacob travels to Haran, finding true love when he meets Rachel and also marries her older sister Leah. He amasses great wealth. And by the end of the Torah portion, Jacob has become a father to twelve children.

But more than that, his Is a journey of development and growth. He leaves behind the deceptive, sneaky approach to life of his youth. He needs to mature, to find himself. This story is about a young man growing a soul, becoming a *mentsch* – a good, kind person. And once he finally develops into that responsible adult, then Jacob is ready to become the great man he is in our tradition. Only after growing, maturing, learning how to be a *mentsch*, does Jacob become a man of faith, ready to wrestle with the angel, and become known as Israel.

That happens only because of what he discovers on the first night of this journey. He takes stones as a pillow and lies down to sleep on the side of the road. That night he has a vision. "He dreamed, and behold there was a *sulam*, a ladder set on the ground with its top reaching to the heavens. And behold, the angels of God went up and down upon it. God stood above and said, 'I am the Holy One, the God of your father Abraham and God of Isaac: I will give the land you lie upon to you and your descendants'" (Gen. 28:12-13). God indeed promises to be with Jacob on his journey of self-discovery, to protect him, and to ensure that his descendants will be blessed throughout the ages, spread out to every part of the world.

When he wakes up from his dream, it is as if his eyes are finally open to an incredible reality in our world: "Behold! The Holy One was in this place and I, I did not know it. How awe-inspiring is this place! This is none other than the house of God, and this is the gate of heaven!" (Gen. 28:16-17).

It's a radical, spiritual declaration to see the sacred in what once seemed ordinary. And it has been a challenge to embrace this important lesson. An old teaching by one of the Hasidic masters embraces this idea. At a Shabbat meal, Rabbi Moshe of Kobryn, the Kobriner Rebbe, once picked up a piece of bread, showed it to his disciples, and taught, "God is here, in this piece of bread. For without God's creative power in all of nature, this bread would not be able to exist."

It's only after Jacob wakes up that he understands. And it is this incredible realization that is an essential reason for us to emulate Jacob as patriarch. His declaration is a beautiful reminder that we need to "wake up," as he did, to God's presence in our lives. Throughout the centuries we have come to understand many different ways we might see the Divine Presence. Perhaps we understand God through the language of science, seeing God's presence in the world of nature, as Baruch Spinoza did. Maybe, like Martin Buber, we come to understand God through an intensely personal, intimate relationship. Perhaps we view God as some invisible guiding force in the universe, a wellspring of energy, and we all are connected to it through our souls, as espoused by Mordecai Kaplan. However we comprehend God, the Presence is right there, waiting to be seen when our eyes are opened. Another great Hasidic master, Menachem Mendl of Kotzk, or the Kotzker Rebbe, famously taught, "Where can God be found? Wherever we let God in."

Jacob opens his eyes, physically and metaphorically, when he wakes and says – "The Holy One was in this place and I did not know it." He leaves from there ready to change, ready to become the father of a nation, knowing God is with him. Jacob reminds us God is everywhere, or nowhere. It just depends on whether or not our eyes are open.

וישלח

——

Vayishlaḥ

Can I Trust You, Brother?

Rabbi Scott Aaron

One of the more maligned of our biblical ancestors is Esau, the eldest son of Isaac and the older brother of Jacob. Most of us recall Esau as the brutish alpha male of Isaac's clan, the one who is described in Genesis 25 as having both a ruddy complexion and red hair. The color red, *adom* in Hebrew, is equated with blood, and much folklore attributes red-headed people as being impulsive and unable to control their tempers and their passions.

Esau is the archetype of this perception. In Genesis 25 he is described as an avid hunter who earns his father's love through his usefulness in providing food for the family. However, in the same chapter, one day after a hunger-inducing hunt, Esau allows himself to be swindled into exchanging his first-born birthright for some of Jacob's lentil soup. Esau's impulsiveness angers his parents despite their love for him when, in Genesis 26, he goes against their wishes and takes two wives from the Hittite tribe rather than from their own kindred tribes. Later, in Genesis 27, the dying Isaac asks Esau for one last meal of his favorite food of venison; Esau goes hunting to provide it for him. Jacob, with the conniving of their mother Rachel, uses Esau's absence and Isaac's failing sight to trick Isaac in to giving the blessing of the first-born to him, thus stealing Esau's spiritual as well as literal birthright. When Esau returns home to find Isaac realizing what had transpired, he begs for his blessing but it is too late. Isaac had but one blessing to give, and he has made Jacob the inheritor of his wealth and his position in the covenant with God. All Isaac can do is give Esau a blessing that states his subservience to his brother, but also gives him permission to rise up against his brother one day to be free of him. Esau, betrayed by his brother and mother, and heartbroken at the imminent loss of his father, impulsively vows to kill his brother once their father is properly buried. This frightens Jacob into running away to his mother's home village.

Time passes and both men become prosperous in their own right, but in Genesis 32-33, Jacob and Esau meet again after Jacob has finally left Laban. Jacob has never forgotten Esau's threat to kill him and, despite his wealth and his own large clan, Jacob fears that Esau's anger has grown worse over the years and that he will slaughter everyone in Jacob's family in revenge. When they finally meet though, Jacob is shocked to find that his brother Esau has matured with the years and no longer holds a grudge against Jacob. Esau greets Jacob warmly and marvels at his family and his success and, to Jacob's astonishment, invites him and his family to settle in Esau's lands as their new home. Old habits die hard though, and while Jacob is relieved at this turn of events, he still tricks Esau one final time. He tells Esau that he will follow behind him as the amount of children and livestock he has requires a slower pace than Esau's group. However, when Esau is safely out of sight, Jacob heads the other way and never joins his brother in his lands. After all, Jacob got where he was in large part due to his ability to trick and swindle, so he naturally assumed Esau either was trying to lure him in to a deathtrap through his offer of a home or was still so naïve that Jacob instinctively lied to him. Either way, the brothers do not settle down as neighbors to raise their families together. The Torah records that they meet only one more time, which is to bury their father, who apparently lived a lot longer than expected.

It is important to note, in Genesis 35, that the Torah does not record any animosity or violence between the two brothers at their father's funeral. Esau apparently had let bygones be bygones and had forgiven Jacob for his behavior from their youth. Yet our tradition largely fails to recognize this maturity and continues to remember Esau primarily as the angry and violent young hunter. Case in point: The descendants of Esau are known as the Edomites, literally the Red Ones or the Bloody Ones, and they are enemies of the biblical monarchy of King David. Our Sages will later posit that the Roman Empire descends from the biblical Edomites, and through the Romans to all of Christianity; this is often cited to explain the horrors of European anti-Semitism throughout post-biblical history. That is a lot of ugliness to hang on to one person. Esau may have been a bit slower than Jacob, differently skilled than Jacob, and even more emotionally impulsive and rebellious than he, but Jacob is the one who behaves unethically at every opportunity towards his brother for his own personal gain. To attribute the origin of centuries of violence towards our people to someone who, when given the opportunity, forgave the wrongs done by his brother to him and let him depart not once but twice from him in peace when he could have easily taken revenge is historically unfair. Esau's story proves that time heals all wounds, and it is time we acknowledge Esau for the good he represents in our historic narrative.

Who Sings in the Almighty's Choir?

Rabbi Yehuda Kelemer

And he (the angel) said: Release me, for the dawn has risen" (Gen. 32:27).

"My time has come to offer song to the Almighty." *Rashi*

A moment of anticipated triumph arrives in the life of our father, Jacob. The trauma of so many years of wandering is about to dissipate, to become dissolved in the exhilarating joy of victory over Esau's adversary, the angel. This adversary pleads to join the Almighty's morning choir. Wouldn't the justifiable response of Jacob be simply a refusal to do so? Couldn't he object by saying: What hypocrisy! Do you really deserve to play an instrument in God's symphony?

Rashi's comment penetrates to the essence of Jacob's mission and is truly a *hashkofic* (theological) somersault. A pyrrhic victory for Esau pales in the face of the discovery of a melody in the sound of every human being, even of an Esau.

At the very moment when well-deserved tranquility is within Jacob's grasp, he is summoned to surrender one dream in order to achieve an even greater one. This is a most unrealistic dream of unusual harmony which for the authentic *tzadik* is the only one worth pursuing, the one which permits the unique song of every living creature to resonate.

Jacob returns to a life in which once again the arena of innumerable challenges increase and yet to the ultimate life of maintaining the vision of a world of: "All mankind will call upon Your Name" (*Aleinu*).

What Is More Important: Materialism or Spirituality?

Bob Margulies

n the opening of *Parashat Vayishlaḥ*, the Torah tells us of how a fearful Jacob was preparing for his upcoming reunion with his twin brother Esau, whom he had not seen in 36 years. The brothers had feuded regarding which one would receive the status of "first born" and which one would receive the special blessings from their father, Isaac. When Jacob received the special blessing after disguising himself in Esau's clothing, Esau threatened to kill Jacob, causing Jacob to flee. Those previous experiences highlighted the different philosophies of life between Jacob and Esau. Here we have their first encounter since then, and to appease Esau's anticipated anger, Jacob prepares lavish gifts to be sent ahead to Esau.

Amazingly, the reunion went well as the brothers hugged, kissed, and met each other's families. During their time together, the Torah highlights a short conversation between the twins which seals the differing philosophies of life, and which contains an important lesson for all of us today.

Esau initially declines the gifts that Jacob sent him stating, "I have a lot [of wealth] — *yesh li rav*" (Gen. 33:9). However, Jacob insists that Esau accept his gifts and says, "Please take my blessing that has been brought to you, for God has been gracious to me, and I have everything – *yesh li kol*" (Gen.33:11). What is the difference between Esau's "I have a lot" and Jacob's "I have everything," and why does Jacob refer to his gifts and wealth as "my blessing"?

The biblical commentator Ramban explains that gifts are referred to as blessing because "he sends from that with which God has blessed him." Jacob refers to his gift as *b'rakha* which emphasizes that, notwithstanding his hard work and effort at business, he recognizes that his success is a blessing from God. Esau, on the other hand, believed that his success was due only to his own efforts and toil. Jacob was always content with what he earned; Esau was always unsatisfied, because no matter how much he possessed, he always wanted more. Esau's philosophy was this: There is always someone richer than I, and I will be unsatisfied until I am richer than the next person.

Unfortunately, by nature many of us tend to never feel content with what we possess. How many people are capable of honestly declaring, as Jacob did, *yesh li kol* – "I have everything" – or of acknowledging that everything they have is a *b'rakha* – a "blessing"? While Esau proclaims "I have a lot," what he really means is that he does not yet have everything. There is always more to acquire, and Esau believed that he had not yet acquired it all. The adage "One who loves money will never be satiated" applies to Esau's mindset: I have a lot, but I always want and need more. In fact, notwithstanding Esau's initial declination of the lavish gifts, he grabbed the gifts immediately after meeting Jacob (Gen. 33:11). His initial declination was nothing more than politics.

According to the commentaries, the root of their different perceptions of wealth was related less to their material outlook and more to their spiritual one. Jacob believed that his physical needs were met completely, irrespective of exactly how much material wealth he really possessed. He appreciated whatever material wealth God gave him and focused on the moral and spiritual good he could do with that wealth. As it is stated in Pirkei Avot 4:1, "Who is rich? He who is happy with his lot," one who graciously accepts whatever God gives him is constantly happy. Such a person does not become caught up in the frustrating pursuit of gaining ever more wealth. Someone who worships money will never have enough and so can never truly be rich. Only one who has an inner sense of contentment and an ongoing partnership with God is really wealthy. This approach to life is the philosophy of Jacob.

Our Jewish tradition certainly encourages education, hard work and effort to attain material goods for our survival and family development. But this *parasha* reminds us that we always need to be mindful that God is our partner in all of our toils, and that if we have the proper mindset of gratitude, graciousness, humility, and contentment with our efforts and possessions, then that will lead to true happiness.

With gratitude to my dear friend, Larry Siegel, who assisted with some of the thoughts herein.

וישב

—

Vayeishev

Think for Yourself

Elias Chajet

The story of Joseph begins long before his birth. His father, Jacob, and his mother, Rachel, had tried and failed for years to have a son. In order to ensure the continuation of the family name, Jacob entered into relationships with many of his servants in hopes that one of them would give birth to a male heir. Jacob was blessed with many sons, but things became problematic when Rachel finally bore Jacob a true male heir.

Anyone who has had kids, has been an older or younger sibling, or has even observed siblings interact, knows what happens when the new child is treated favorably by parents. Older siblings tend to become jealous. When the younger sibling's arrogance is tossed into the mix, as was the case for Joseph, jealousy turns to animosity. The magnitude of hatred and animosity toward Joseph peaks when he describes and interprets a dream to his brothers. In this dream, Joseph saw a field of wheat bowing down to one stalk in the center. Joseph interpreted this to mean that one day, his entire family would bow down to him as their ruler.

When presented with only one controversial interpretation of Joseph's dream, his brothers did what a majority of the millennial population would do: They allowed his interpretation to become their belief. Unfortunately for Joseph, his brothers' belief in his interpretation caused them to act irrationally by throwing Joseph into a pit before selling him to a band of passing traders.

Classical Jewish ethics and character development aid us in understanding that each individual has his or her own opposite extremes. These extreme opposites can include traits such as pride and humility, generosity and stinginess, mercy and cruelty, as well as any other character trait one can imagine. These polar extremes are evident in three types of people, and all are seen among Joseph and his brothers. The first type of person is one who follows natural, primal instincts. Second, there is an individual known as an elevated person – someone whose actions are dictated by intellect and thought. This type of human responds to good deeds with subsequent kindness and good deeds while responding to evil and hatred with more evil and hatred. Third is the individual known as the *Rasha* or evildoer. This is an individual who defers to immoral or unethical people and tries to be accepted into their society. On the other hand, this person disparages those who are righteous and good. Unfortunately for

Joseph, his brothers' personalities include minute aspects of the elevated person paired with stronger traits of the follower and of the *Rasha*.

Joseph acted as the elevated soul, living day-to-day life on the dictates of his intellect. He, as the youngest son, served his father Jacob as well as his brothers, who are of a lower status because of their births to handmaidens. It seems that Joseph's life goal was to better those around him, although no good deed goes unpunished. Joseph would interpret his dreams in an effort to "teach wise conduct to his brothers." Joseph would tell his brothers of dreams that signified their eventual servitude to him. Although Joseph's goal was not to offend and belittle his brothers, that was the result.

This part of the story is where interpretation itself is key to understanding and is a major turning point for Joseph as well as the Jewish people. It is not Joseph's interpretation or opinion of dreams that is problematic. It is his brothers' lack of interpretation that leads to Joseph's ultimate demise. Similar to the way a millennial would respond to a controversial Facebook or Twitter post, Joseph's brothers took one interpretation and turned it into their belief. Acting as the first type of human described above, Joseph's brothers acted instinctively after blindly believing in Joseph's dream. They did not think to question or interpret his dream in their own way. Luckily for Joseph, his brothers had a change of heart and instead of killing him, sold him to a band of Ishmaelite traders. This allowed Joseph to continue to interpret dreams, resulting in his success in Egypt, albeit a temporary success.

Throughout the twentieth- and twenty-first centuries, humanity has taken enormous progressive strides toward equality, technological advances that were inconceivable fifty years ago, and conservation of our amazing planet, among other phenomenal advancements. Unfortunately it seems that society has forgotten the importance of personal interpretation and belief. In a highly technological world where all forms of information are available at one's fingertips, it seems as if we as a society have forgotten how to read through an article to form an opinion. Perhaps it is because of decreasing attention spans, increased laziness, or just a lack of time, millennials read a headline and the first paragraph of an article. In turn, that small section of an article becomes the individual's opinion. It is much too common an occurrence that an individual speaks or acts without questioning, just as Joseph's brothers did. Just as they acted on Joseph's interpretation of his own dream without thinking critically about the validity of his comments, modernity has shown us that accepting interpretations as fact without generating one's own opinion is the norm and acceptable. Humanity must strive to correct this, to become an elevated society which acts on dictates of its intellect and critical thinking, not on blind faith, following, or understanding.

The Gift of Tears

Rabbi Andrew Jacobs

"And he kissed all his brothers and wept over them" (Gen. 45:15)

The ability to cry is a gift from God. Washington Irving, the great American author, wrote:

> There is a sacredness in tears. They are not the mark of weakness, but of power. They speak more eloquently than ten thousand tongues. They are the messengers of over-whelming grief, of deep contrition, and of unspeakable love.

Irving's words have been backed up by science. Dr. Oren Hasson, an evolutionary biologist at Tel Aviv University, has proven that crying brings people together, strengthening relationships. "Emotional tears," Hasson states, are "a validation of emotions among family, friends and members of a group." Crying connects us to the people in our lives. So, imagine if you could not cry.

In December 2013, the world mourned the passing of Nelson Mandela, the anti-apartheid leader who served as South Africa's president from 1994 to 1999. Because of his leadership role in the struggle against the racial segregation of apartheid, Mandela was imprisoned in late 1962. It was not until early 1990 that he was released. After more than 27 years in prison, Mandela continued to fight, using his freedom to stand up to apartheid once again. He successfully negotiated with South African political leaders to form a multiracial government. It was by no means an easy process, but it led to the end of apartheid and earned Mandela and then-president of South Africa, F. W. de Klerk, the Nobel Peace Prize in 1993. The following year, the first multiracial election in South Africa's history was held, and Mandela became the country's president.

As the world mourned Mandela's passing in December 2013, United States President Obama, Israeli Prime Minister Netanyahu, leaders from the European Union, and countless others spoke out to express their sadness and, at the same time, commend Mandela's accom-plishments. The tribute that touched me the most was written by the singer and activist Bono. He wrote a powerful eulogy for Mandela in *Time* magazine, praising the courage and strength of the late leader while also focusing on the fact that Mandela was not able to cry. As a result of being forced to work long hours in a limestone mine while in prison, Mandela's tear ducts were severely damaged by dust.

The damage left him unable to shed a tear. Bono writes that as a result of Mandela's captivity, he was flawed: "For all this man's farsightedness and vision, he could not produce tears in a moment of self-doubt or grief."

Many might argue that Mandela's inability to cry was not worth mentioning in a eulogy, particularly since we often see tears as a sign of weakness, and Mandela was by no means a weak man. But Bono knew that if Mandela could have wept, he would have wept, and his weeping would not have been a sign of weakness. It would have been a sign that he was able to express himself freely with those he loved and those who loved him. Thus, even after being released from jail and given the freedom again to fight apartheid, Mandela's inability to cry was a sign of his prolonged captivity.

In *Parashat Vayeishev* we read about Joseph, another great leader who had a challenging life. His brothers treated him terribly and tossed him into a pit, which resulted in him being sold into slavery and transported to Egypt. Over time, however, Joseph would overcome his challenges and rise to power in Egypt as he gained the trust and admiration of Pharaoh. Many years later, a plague destroyed the produce of Israel and Joseph's brothers came to Egypt in search of food. They found themselves standing before their extremely powerful brother, who forgives them, embraces them and, as he does so, cries. In doing so, Joseph reconnects with his brothers and heals the shattered relationships that tore the family apart. Joseph's tears are not a sign of weakness. They are a sign of his strength and determination to connect with his family, lead them from the darkness of the past, and guide them toward a brighter future.

Soon after becoming South Africa's president, Mandela had corrective surgery that would allow him to cry. In doing so, Mandela was teaching Torah. As the leader of the nation he loved deeply, he needed to be able to cry because, as Washington Irving taught us, tears are how we express our "unspeakable love." It was only by ending his captivity once and for all and allowing himself to express his emotions freely that Mandela, like Joseph, could lead his people toward a brighter future.

The ability to cry is a gift from God.

It's All in the Trope

Stuart Tauber

Many of us are aware that when the Torah is read aloud in synagogue each week a trope, a cantillation, is available to the reader in order to provide listeners with greater insight into events taking place in the unfolding story. It often provides a "sitting at the edge of your seat" sound track through which those in the congregation can empathize with a story character in a manner no less powerful than that which comes from a musical score accompanying one of today's modern movies or plays.

One of the most difficult of the various tropes is known as a *shalshelet*. The *shalshelet* rises in various octaves and frequencies and then just stops. It is a rarely used cantillation probably because of the difficulty in getting it right. I have laughed to myself on the many occasions when those *laining* (reading the Torah aloud for the congregation) deliberately use a self-invented version of the *shalshelet* trope so as to improve the flow without mangling the actual reading. As rare as it is, however, the trope is nonetheless found on at least three different occasions in Genesis alone. If we take a moment to examine its usage, we can gain greater clarity of the attempted seduction of Joseph by Potiphar's wife in *Parashat Vayeishev*.

Shalshelet 1: In the story of Sodom and Gomorrah, God's angels tell Lot to take his family and flee the land before it is destroyed. The morning he was to leave, however, the Torah records *vayitmahmeah* ("and he lingered"), utilizing the *shalshelet* trope. Lot hesitated. As immoral as the town may have become, Lot had become a wealthy citizen. His sons-in-law who worked with him in the family business wanted to stay. They all were living the good life, and Lot was very tempted to remain in Sodom. Biblical legend has it that the angels actually had to push Lot out of town.

Shalshelet 2: In *Parashat Vayeira*, Abraham is hoping to find a wife for his son Isaac. Abraham sends his trusted servant Eliezer out, charged with the task of finding the right woman. Having some difficulty, Eliezer speaks to God: *Vayomar* ("and he said"), also accompanied by the *shalshelet* trope. Eliezer begs God to send him the right woman. Biblical commentators tell us that Eliezer, like Lot, was also tempted. It seems Eliezer had a daughter of his own. How wonderful it would have been to tell Abraham the only good match would be between his daughter and Abraham's son? Instead Eliezer prayed that God would connect him with the true perfect wife for Isaac.

These two different stories share destiny-altering decisions for the Jewish people. Both Eliezer and Lot wanted to choose the easier path, one they perceived as more self-satisfying and enriching. Instead they chose the more difficult but morally correct one. Had they not, Jewish destiny would have been altered dramatically. If Lot remained in Sodom, his eldest daughter would not have given birth to her son Moab. That would be the same Moab whose descendants would include Ruth and King David. If Eliezer had not made the connection between Isaac and Rebekah there would have been no Jacob and no twelve tribes. Clearly the *shalshelet* was meant to tell the reader that Lot and Eliezer were facing destiny-altering decisions that would only be revealed to the Jewish people in the future.

So on to Joseph. Potiphar's beautiful wife is very attracted to him. She attempts to seduce him. The Torah tells us, however, *Vayema'aine* ("he refused her advances"), and above the refusal, the all-telling *shalshelet*. Contrary to popular belief, this was no quick refusal by a morally superior human being. Joseph was very tempted. Who wouldn't have been? Like Lot, he too, hesitated. Then he made the destiny-altering choice to flee. Had he not, Potiphar's wife might never have accused him of the rape, setting into motion the chain of events that would eventually lead him to become the Vice Pharaoh. Had he not reached that exalted position, the Jews might never have ended up as slaves in Egypt.

Too bad music is not piped into our lives from the sky as it is in the movies. Perhaps each time we were faced with decisions that would alter our destiny, we would hear the sound of the *shalshelet* warning us: "Take care. Don't take the easy way out." We all know that more often than not in life, the easy way out is not the path we should be taking. Great rewards come with great challenges but only when we listen for the internal sound of the *shalshelet*.

I would be remiss if I did not take a moment to remember my father, Rabbi Jack Tauber z"l, with gratitude for teaching me to layin, *to correctly chant the* shalshelet *and, more importantly, to appreciate the meaning of this unique and rare trope.*

מקץ

— — —

Mikkeitz

Problem Solved

Bruce A. Lev

This *parasha* relates the miraculous story of how Joseph rose from the depths of being a prisoner in Egypt to the heights of a position of leadership in the greatest empire of the ancient world.

We see three attributes for which Joseph became well known:

First we learn about his own dreams as a young man, when his brothers' bundles of wheat bowed down to his bundles, and then the sun, the moon, and eleven stars bowed down to him.

Second, his uncommon skill at interpreting dreams comes out in this *parasha* as he interprets the dreams of his fellow prison-mates, the butler and the baker.

Finally, the most important trait of a great leader is being solution oriented, rather than just complaining about a problem or identifying it without solving it. Joseph teaches us about his wonderful knack of bringing solutions to the table for the problem at hand. Most people complain about problems and leave them for others to resolve. Not Joseph. He exhibits his excellent leadership skills in this *parasha* when he interprets Pharaoh's dream to mean the seven years of plenty would be followed by seven years of famine. He then presents a solution to Pharaoh's problem as follows:

> Now let Pharaoh look for a discerning and wise man and put him in charge of the land of Egypt. Let Pharaoh appoint commissioners over the land to take a fifth of the harvest of Egypt during the seven years of abundance. They should collect all the food of these good years that are coming and store up the grain under the authority of Pharaoh, to be kept in the cities for food. This food should be held in reserve for the country to be used during the seven years of famine that will come upon Egypt, so that the country may not be ruined by the famine (Gen. 41:33-36).

It should be noted that this recommendation to Pharaoh about how to solve this seemingly insurmountable problem came unsolicited from Joseph. Pharaoh's request was simply to interpret his dreams. Joseph took the request an important step further and showed his leadership skills by coming up with a solution which was easily adopted by Pharaoh. Joseph's initiative ultimately led to his attaining a leadership position in the Egyptian government.

We learn from this episode how easy it it is to complain about things in our lives, both large and small. Wouldn't the world be a better place if there was an attitude of being solution oriented like Joseph, solving challenges at hand, whether in our personal, work, or communal lives?

We see another example of this unsolicited problem-solving approach later on in Exodus, in *Parashat Yitro*. Moses' father-in-law, Jethro, saw what Moses was doing and said:

> *What is this thing that you are doing to the people? Why do you sit by yourself, while all the people stand before you from morning until evening?…The thing that you are doing is not good…You should appoint God-fearing men, and they will judge the people on a full-time basis. When a major item arises, they will bring it to you, but the minor matters they will judge themselves. This will make it easier for you, for they will bear the burden with you* (Exod. 18:14-22).

Instead of stopping with the complaint and just stating the problem, Jethro recommended a solution. He told Moses to appoint good leaders and let them judge the many cases. This would free Moses from such time-consuming activities and allow him to focus on more important things on behalf of the community. This was the world's first lesson in time management, long before electronic calendars and to-do lists.

We see from both Joseph, and later Jethro, that either being a problem solver or surrounding oneself with problem solvers is the sign of a good leader. May we take this much-needed concept to heart in our daily lives and follow in these exemplary footsteps as shown in this wonderful *parasha, Mikkeitz.*

My Dreams,
Your Interpretations

Rabbi Michael Paley

"All that we see or seem is but a dream within a dream." *Edgar Allen Poe*

This *parasha* is a dream within dreams. We find Pharaoh, dreaming of standing by the Nile watching thin cows eat fat cows and thin grain swallowing solid and healthy grain. He wakes up and asks, "But what could the dreams mean?" I have always found the next lines the most puzzling. Pharaoh sends for all the wise men and psychologists of Egypt and no one could interpret the dream. Is the dream that hard? I feel as though even I could have given a satisfying understanding! They needed Joseph, the Israelite who held the Divine spirit, to unravel the meaning. After a haircut and a change of clothes, Joseph is brought to the court and the Pharaoh tells him the long story of the dreams; Joseph immediately explains them. Just like that. How? Well, Dr. Freud, are Jews just better at understanding dreams?

To answer this and other questions we have to go back a bit, to *Parashat Vayeishev* (Gen. 37) where we find the 17-year-old Joseph, an annoying teenager with parental support for his fashion statement. Joseph is the oldest son of Rachel, the second wife of Jacob. He is smart, handsome, and loved – you know the type. He also had some dreams of his own and is living "a dream within a dream." Noting that his brothers hate him, he decides to share the content of his controversial and provocative dreams. Joseph dreamed that he was with his brothers, binding sheaves in the field when his bundle stood up and theirs all seemed to bow down. The brothers interpreted the dream to mean that eventually they would bow down to Joseph (Gen. 37:7). Of course this comes true later in our section (Gen. 42:6). Relevant here is that everyone thought that they knew what the first dream meant. The second dream was similar and simple: The sun, the moon, and 11 stars were bowing down to Joseph. Even Jacob, sure in his interpretation, berated Joseph for telling everyone this dream (Gen. 37:10).

But did they understand the two dreams correctly? If the interpretation of the dreams was so obvious, why did Joseph tell them? Suppose the brothers got Joseph's dreams wrong? Suppose the dreams were not about Joseph at all, not about his grandeur or even his power? Maybe the dreams were more straightforward. Perhaps the first one was not about Joseph but simply about grain flopping down in a future famine. The second dream has 13 astronomical objects, one for each year until the start of the famine cycle, which would begin with years of plenty. If that was the nature of the dreams then it was about survival and not ego. If the famine, according to the dreams, was to start in 13 years, it would mean Joseph would be 30 years old when the famine cycle would start, plenty of time to prepare if you knew what was coming.

Back to *Mikkeitz*. We are told that Joseph entered into the service of the Pharaoh when he was 30 years old. Instead of being at home and storing grain, he had been in an Egyptian prison. The 13 years had passed, just as the second dream told him through the use of the sun, moon, and 11 stars. How did he understand Pharaoh's dreams so quickly? He had spent a considerable amount of those 13 years in pits, dungeons and jails, giving him plenty of time to reconsider all that had happened and to let his anger build. He had been waiting for many years to hear the Pharaoh's dreams, and now he had the control to stop the famine, almost as a bonus. If the brothers had only understood that his dreams weren't about power, but that a famine was coming, it would have been different for them and for us.

Much of this portion foreshadows the story of Queen Esther. Both Joseph and Esther are good-looking Jewish kids in a diaspora who get cleaned up before they see the king. Both kings seem to like them in different ways, and they use their courage and imagination to save the Jews. But this does not come without some interior struggle. Esther doesn't want to go see the king and if not for Mordechai, who like Joseph is led around on a horse dressed like the king and wearing his ring, she would not have gone (Esther 4). Joseph is even more conflicted.

Like Esther, whose real name is Hadassah, Joseph gets an Egyptian name and an Egyptian wife who bore him two sons. The first son was named Menashe, and we are told that it means, "God has made me completely forget my suffering and the house of my father." In other words, "I hate my family!" But the second son he named Ephraim, which we are told means, "God has blessed me with abundance in the land of my affliction." Significantly Joseph understands Egypt to be an alien place even though he is in charge. This is Joseph's dilemma: Is he at home in Egypt or is he alone, understood or a stranger, done with the past or always in service of it? He will not know the answer until his brothers show up to get food for their families and bow down before him.

On Friday nights the tradition is to bless our sons with the phrase, "like Ephraim and like Menashe." But who wants their son to feel like the name Menashe, "I hate my family"? When Jacob was dying and reunited with Joseph, he asked to bless Joseph's sons. He knew to cross his hands and bless the younger one first so that with all the misinterpretations behind him, he could remind Joseph he was blessed with abundance but not yet out of the land of his affliction.

All in the Family

Rabbi Noam Raucher

Here is a story about a family dilemma. A student of mine, Sandy, converted to Judaism. Shortly after doing so, she flew home to Spain to share the news of the conversion with her family. Sandy was so excited to tell them how she had found a meaningful spiritual practice. As soon as the taxi pulled up to her home she was greeted with hugs and kisses from her parents and siblings. Immediately the family sat down to a big dinner. The meal was composed of savory dishes, and at the center was a giant roasted pig with an apple in its mouth.

Sandy was shocked. In her excitement to join the Jewish people she had immersed herself in Jewish practice. She loved the peace and quiet of Shabbat. She reflected intensely when she prayed in synagogue. And she loved cooking kosher meals. In her zeal to convert she accidentally forgot some of the traditions of her birthplace. Needless to say, Sandy didn't know what to do. Here she was, ready to tell her family about her new life, hoping for their love, and in the same breath she would have to tell them she could not eat the food they had prepared specifically for her visit!

Feeling anxious she excused herself for a moment to think. While doing so she remembered how much she missed her family and how she longed to see them. She knew that the distance she had created by building a life for herself in the United States strained their relationships. She wanted to be with them just like it was when she was a kid, laughing around the dinner table while telling stories. But she also wanted to be Jewish. She felt proud of her decision to become a Jew and wanted to live an active Jewish life. But she knew that if she didn't participate in the meal, her parents certainly would be upset. And that was the last thing she wanted to cause during her visit home.

After what seemed like a long bathroom break she returned to dinner. As she sat down she saw a plate of food prepared for her with all the options from the table. As she felt what it was like to sit with her family once again she closed her eyes, took a deep breath, said the traditional blessing over a meal, and took her first bite.

When Sandy came back to the States she met with me to talk about her visit. She told me how she felt simultaneously great about her visit with family and guilty that she had abandoned her Jewish convictions during the meal. She said her family welcomed her choice to be Jewish. They praised her for finding a spiritual path which gave her fulfillment, even if they didn't completely understand what it required. I reminded her that her parents were still her parents even if they were not Jewish. And that Judaism asks that she still honor them for that reason. But I also told her that while eating those meals with her family she actually lived out a very important Jewish value. I told her about the concept of *shalom bayit*, a peaceful home.

I told her the story of Joseph and how he had a difficult family life. After all, his brothers sold him into slavery. However, when Joseph sees his brothers again – after years of separation – something had changed in all of them. He could have pretended that he didn't know who they were and denied them outright. He could have let the differences between them fester and push them further apart. Instead he took a different tack. He recognized that his brothers had changed and had become men of virtue. And in turn, Joseph decided to drop his guard so they could see their lost brother. In so doing they created a *shalom bayit*, a peaceful home. From then on his family lived together in prosperity.

Family is no exception to the messiness of life. People change and grow. They develop their own sense of self and identity. Sometimes that is at odds with other people in our families who have done the same. For some these are points of contention. But Sandy – and Joseph and his brothers – teach us that there is something more important: to be able to dwell together. To accomplish that we must be willing to relinquish our own priorities and meet each other half way for the sake of an even greater priority: peace in our homes. As the psalmist teaches: How good and pleasant it is when brothers and sisters dwell together (Ps. 133:1). How good indeed.

ויגש

—

Vayiggash

Finding a Place to Think

Bob Margulies

I n *Parashat Vayiggash*, the Torah tells of the descent of Jacob and the tribes to Egypt and the designation of their dwelling place as "the land of Goshen." It seems that Joseph intentionally desired that his family and people settle in the Egyptian province of Goshen, as the Torah states: "Yosef said to his brothers ... when Pharaoh summons you ... Then you are to say, 'Your servants have been cattlemen'... so that you may be able to settle on the land of Goshen." So it was, "Israel settled in the land of Egypt in the land of Goshen; they acquired property in it and they were fruitful and multiplied greatly" (Gen. 46-47).

What was special about that place called "the land of Goshen," and why was Joseph so keen on settling his families in this place?

The simple understanding is that this place was far from the Egyptian population, to be separate from the Egyptians and not to be influenced by Egyptian culture. Therefore, Joseph sought to settle his brothers there. The famous biblical commentator, Rabbi Shlomo Ephraim Luntschitz (*Kli Yakar*), the rabbi of Prague in the early 17th century, writes: "The purpose of all of this was to distance them from Pharaoh, so that they would settle in the land of Goshen." Another prominent commentator with this view, Rabbi Naftali Tzvi Yehuda Berlin (*Netziv*), a 19th-century rabbi in what is now Belarus, states that Joseph wanted his brothers to live in isolation in order to preserve their purity, even though this would arouse the hatred of the Egyptians. In an interesting comment, the esteemed 19th-century German rabbi, Samson Raphael Hirsch, despite his stated preference for synthesis of the Torah world and the secular world (*Torah im Derekh Eretz* – the precursor to today's "Modern Orthodox"), attempts to explain the rationale for this approach based on the historical reality:

> The disgust of the Egyptians for their profession...was the first means of preservation of the race which was destined for an isolated path throughout the ages...That is why Joseph acted with the express purpose of obtaining a separate province within which his family would settle. As long as the ethical dawn of the other nations had not yet come, it was the partitions that the other nations erected which preserved Israel from being infected by the corruption of the people among whom it dwelled for hundreds of years (Commentary to Gen. 46:33).

Other commentaries attempt to explain this decision in terms of the negative effects that city dwelling has on a person's spiritual growth. Another esteemed biblical commentator, Don Isaac Abravanel (1437-1508), wrote that shepherding provides a simple, humble, and sacred alternative to living among those in positions of authority and power. The distinguished scholar, Rabbeinu Bachaya of Spain (1255-1340), argues (in his commentary to Gen. 46:32) that shepherding offers three major benefits: (a) It produces necessary and important materials (meat, wool, milk) for relatively little effort; (b) Given the low status of shepherding in Egypt, the brothers would have a monopoly on this profession; and (c) Because it involves seclusion, shepherds were not only able to avoid the damaging gossip and talebearing that personify so many human interactions, they were also able to find time for self-examination and spiritual growth.

Whatever approach you find more appealing in understanding Joseph's motivation in settling the family in the land of Goshen, the beloved 20th-century biblical scholar and commentator, Nehama Leibowitz (1905-1997), points out "unfortunately they still became enmeshed in the attractions of the surrounding society and forgot the temporary nature of their sojourn in Egypt." The last verse of our *parasha* alludes to the dangers of assimilation when it states, "and Israel settled in the land of Egypt and in the land of Goshen; they acquired holdings therein and were fruitful and increased greatly in numbers" (Gen. 47:27).

This a lesson for all generations, as Moses Maimonides (the Rambam, 1135-1204), one of the greatest Jewish thinkers, writes in his Mishneh Torah (*Hilchot Deiyot* 6:1): "The nature of man is to be drawn in his thoughts and actions after his companions and friends, to act like the people of his nation. Therefore, a person has to join the righteous and to sit always in their presence so that he will learn from their actions." This is what King Solomon (*Shlomo HaMelech*) said: "One, who walks with the wise, will grow wise, but the companion of fools will be broken" (Prov. 13:20). It further says, "Praiseworthy is the man who walked not in the counsel of the wicked...But his desire is in the Torah of the Lord, and in his Torah he meditates day and night."

It is very difficult to buck the trend, to be your own person and do the ethical and proper thing, when sometimes it seems that "everyone else" is doing the "wrong" thing. But to grow and develop into a righteous person often requires a separation from the herd, from the masses, and from the crowd. Sometimes the separation may be spiritual and not only physical; it may be just a state of mind as much as a state of the heart. All of us at times may need to have our own private "Goshen" where we can contemplate right from wrong, ethical vs. unethical, and grow in spirituality in a location somewhat insulated from the secular, materialistic forces which surround us.

Joseph speaks to us today. May we heed his message for our own spiritual growth and development. "The nature of man is to be drawn in his thoughts and actions after his companions and friends, to act like the people of his nation. Therefore, a person has to join the righteous and to sit always in their presence so that he will learn from their actions."

Approaching God

Rabbi Lyle Rothman

Each time I enter the synagogue of my youth, the words *"Da lifnei mi atah omed* – Know before whom you stand" shine down upon me from above the *aron kodesh* – the Holy Ark. Although this phrase from rabbinic literature is inscribed on countless sanctuaries, can we ever truly understand what these words express? How can we begin to approach and stand vulnerably before God?

Our biblical ancestors constantly were charged with the task of approaching challenging situations, yet the verb *vayiggash* – "he approached" – is found only three times in the Torah. Abraham boldly approaches God when he learns that Sodom and Gemorah are going to be destroyed (Gen. 18:23). Elijah approaches God in a confrontation on Mount Carmel with the false prophets of Baal (1 Kings 18:36-37). As our *parasha* begins, Judah approaches his brother Joseph (*vayiggash eilav Yehudah*) and pleads for the release of their brother Benjamin (Gen. 44:18). Each time the biblical writer employs the word *vayiggash*, a prayer is uttered and lives are changed. These prayerful *vayiggash* moments helped our biblical ancestors approach difficult situations, and they can help us learn how to enter into a relationship with the Divine.

Rabbi Menachem Mendel of Kotzk, a great Ḥassidic teacher, once asked his students, "Where does God dwell?" The students answered that "God lives everywhere." The Kotzker Rebbe was not satisfied with their answer. While it may be true that God lives everywhere, he taught, "God dwells wherever people let Him in." Once we begin to approach God, ultimately we must be willing to truly let Him in to our lives.

It was Shabbat somewhere between evening and morning – 3:15 am, to be exact – and I approached God. My alarm went off, and I looked around the room confused. I saw a small crucifix hanging on the wall to my right, and to my left was a wood carving of St. Agnes. I quickly got dressed and put on my Shabbat kippah. As I walked outside, I was greeted by the sounds of crickets and the darkest night sky illuminated by thousands of stars. I took a moment to look around and take in the beauty – God is surely in this place and I do know it. I made my way into the church for vigils, a communal praying of the psalms. As I entered, I paused to take note of the large stained glass window of the Virgin Mary holding the baby Jesus. I began to feel uncomfortable. Why am I in a church in the middle of the night on Shabbat?

It's now 3:30 am, and the monks make their way into the church. The sound of feet along the wood floorboards grows louder. One of the monks ascends to the prayer table in the middle of the room, hits the table, and they start to pray a familiar psalm. The words "God open my lips that my mouth may declare Your praise" come forth from their mouths in a strange yet calming chant – Gregorian chant. Two more times those words are repeated and now the monk community is ready to pray.

I felt a sense of familiarity with the words, and yet the people surrounding me were not like me. I can't really tell you what happened next, but I sat there for 45 minutes soaking in the sounds of sacred words. When vigils were concluded, one of the monks made his way to the front of the church and we were splashed with holy water. The water droplets flew across the room and hit me unexpectedly. I was a stranger in a strange land, and I immediately felt vulnerable.

For the next day and a half, I immersed myself in the monastic life-style as a retreatant at Saint Joseph's Abbey in Spencer, Massachusetts, a Trappist monastery. I found opportunities to approach God while being strengthened by that cloistered Catholic community. The vulnerability that I felt in the early hours of the morning after suddenly being splashed by holy water remained with me. Yet it is that vulnerability that continues to strengthen my faith today.

Rabbi Jonathan Sacks teaches "Faith is the ability to rejoice in the midst of change and instability, traveling through the wilderness of time towards an unknown destination." This vulnerability is a blessing, one that we can learn to embrace. Who among us has not felt the loneliness of vulnerability – the feeling of no one to share our dreams with and the challenges to others that went unheard? Yes it is true: Vulnerability is often seen as something negative. But in light of our Jewish past, when we journeyed through the great unknown, perhaps we can begin to see vulnerability as being true to our authentic selves.

As the former Director of Jewish Life and Learning at Hofstra Hillel, I saw young adults as they journeyed between sorrow and happiness. For this age group, sorrow may be breaking up with a first love or failing a class. Happiness may be getting the coveted internship or getting into graduate school. All of these highs and lows undoubtedly make our students feel vulnerable and sometimes very alone. But as their rabbi, one of my main responsibilities was to nurture their souls, to listen to their dreams, to hear their challenges, and to respond to their calls for help. Even at times of change and instability, our young adults need to find new and creative ways to approach God.

For our ancestors, their *vayiggash* moments helped them prayerfully approach God. My *vayiggash* moment encouraged me to vulnerably seek God in unlikely places. Together may our souls be nourished and energized by the uncertainty of what the future holds. Lord, give us the strength to be vulnerable when approaching You. Please help us to open our lips so our mouths can declare Your praise in joy. Only then will we truly know before whom we stand.

And You Thought *Your* Family Was Dysfunctional?

Stuart Tauber

Though embarrassed to admit it, I am addicted to Showtime's television series *Shameless*. For the unfamiliar, the storyline centers on an extremely poor family and their "shameless" behavior. The father, an ever-willing-to-work, drug-addicted alcoholic regularly steals rent money from his children. The kids sell drugs, steal goods, lie to police, rip off neighbors and friends, etc., etc. Though the children love one another, their behavior is so immoral that the most forgiving of viewers still have no trouble recognizing the depravity of the situation.

This brings me to thoughts of my own folks. Growing up, I was proud of my family roots. Dad was a prominent community rabbi. During the Holocaust he smuggled Jews out of Europe and brought them to America. He was a gun runner for Israel in the early days of the state's creation. My mom was also a terrific individual. She grew up in a small town, the daughter of a rabbi. While dad was the house scholar, mom was the one who taught me to ride a bike, drive a car (with a clutch), and with lightning speed take apart a kitchen sink in need of plumbing repair. Both parents were well-respected by the neighbors. So much so that on occasion, when my brothers or I misbehaved at school, in synagogue, or summer camp, we knew we would coast through the challenge on the wings of the good feelings people had for the folks.

Yup, no doubt about it, I think most people like having parents whom they know are kind, respected, loving, and so on. A thought that should be kept in mind when reading *Parashat Vayiggash*. In the *parashiyot* leading up to *Vayiggash* we were introduced to our forefather Jacob, his wives, and the kids. To be kind, I cannot imagine anyone ever wanting to admit they were part of this family. These are, well, the original "shameless" bunch. Jacob who stole a birthright from his older brother. Jacob who treated his first wife miserably. (No matter how many kids she gave him he couldn't find a way to even fake a scintilla of affection for her.) A father who let all the kids know that he had a favorite. (Whew!) And how about those kids? Jealous of their younger brother (Joseph), they debate whether to kill him or just sell him into slavery. They lied to their father Jacob and told him their brother – his son – had been killed.

Just when we think this family can't get anymore dysfunctional we come to *Vayiggash*, where the crescendo is building. We learn that 20 years after lying to their father, the kids still haven't told him the truth that their brother is alive. They let dad go all these years with the pain of believing he outlived his favorite son. (What kind of people can hold a secret like that for so long knowing the level of pain it caused their father?) And how about Joseph? He does not seem much better than the rest of the clan. He has gone on to become one of the most powerful people on the face of the Earth and yet has apparently felt no need to send even a single soldier under his command in search of his father. No need to let dad know he is still alive. No need to visit with him for a couple of decades either. (There are rabbis who believe that because this was part of God's plan, the Lord blocked the feelings in Joseph that would have changed his behavior. I don't buy it. Apple trees don't grow oranges. They grow little apples.)

So I ask you. Would you want to admit you were part of this family? And yet…we Jews proudly speak of our roots and connection to this branch of the family tree. In fact, we congratulate ourselves on being the descendants of Jacob and family. (There are those in our midst who pray in the traditional Jewish manner multiple times each day emphasizing that connection.) All of this should make for a lot of wondering on our part. "What was the Lord thinking when hatching a plan making this family the foundation of a chosen Hebrew people?" Was this shameless group the best God could find?

Yet at that moment when I think we shouldn't be so quick to claim our birthright alongside this particular cast of characters, I find comfort in knowing they had so many human frailties. If such a family and group of individuals could serve as the foundation of a proud faith and nation, imagine what the rest of us, those who lead far more moral lives, can achieve if we just put our minds to it. Perhaps God was trying tell us that if this very challenged family could go on to find enormous success in the realm of our Creator, the rest of us with just a minimal amount of effort (helping the poor, speaking out on behalf of the powerless, protecting the vulnerable) can truly be exceptional people in that same spiritual realm.

וַיְחִי

Vayeḥi

The Blessing of Memories

Rabbi Daniel Bar-Nahum

"Should old acquaintance be forgot, and never brought to mind? Should old acquaintance be forgot, for auld lang syne?" Many of us sing these words every year on New Year's Eve, not really knowing what it is we're singing about. Most of the words are in English: "Should old acquaintance be forgot and never brought to mind." That seems to make sense, but then at the end of the second line we sing: "for auld lang syne." What does that mean? Where does it come from? The song was authored by a Scot named Robert Burns in 1788. But the idiomatic phrase, "auld lang syne," predates him by at least 200 years; even Burns claimed that this poem was an old Scottish folk song, finally put to paper by him.

Rav Google informs us that the phrase "auld lang syne" can be translated as "old long since," but makes more sense as "for old time's sake." So, "Should old acquaintance be forgot for auld lang syne?" "Should we forget our old friends?" the lyrics ask. What about those times that we shared, good and bad? What about the things that we learned together? What about the friends that we made? What about all our memories? As we wind down a year, it makes sense to look back on what was.

Vayehi, the last *parasha* of the book of Genesis, is read around the secular New Year's Eve. The *parasha* describes the sons of Jacob gathering at their father's deathbed: "Jacob called to his sons, saying: 'Gather round so that I may tell you what will befall to you in days to come'" (Gen. 49:1). "Gather round," Jacob tells his children. Reunite here, as I lie on the precipice of life and death and look to the future. But while Jacob asks them to look forward, the sons cannot help but look back. In some readings of the poem that makes up Jacob's last testament, Jacob speaks to his sons individually. In other interpretations he speaks of the distant future, speaking not to his sons, but to the tribes their names represent. Jacob's purpose is clear: He gathers his sons together to look to the future, knowing that they will also look back to their past.

Our ability to remember what was is itself a blessing. We get to think back to the times that we shared with loved ones, laughing and joking. We also are blessed with the ability to look back at the difficulties that we may have had and see how much we have grown and how much we may have put behind us in order to move forward.

By looking back, we understand where we are now and how we're going to move ahead.

Though *Vayehi* provides a literal blessing from Jacob to his sons upon his death, we see the blessing of memory more so in actions and words, particularly those of Joseph. Joseph's brothers fear his retribution after their father's death. They look back and see that they were not the best brothers, what with selling him into slavery and staging his death. For them this reunion is an opportunity to make amends. They proclaim to Joseph that they are ready to serve him as slaves. Joseph looks back. He remembers. But he focuses not on the fact that his brothers wronged him, but that they are his brothers. He calmly says to them: "'Have no fear, I will sustain you and your children.' He reassured them and spoke to their hearts" (Gen. 50:21). In coming together with his brothers, he recalls the past; he understands it but recognizes the importance of the present and the future. In the past they were enemies. At present, they are mourning their father. In the future, their family's survival is at stake. Joseph puts aside ill feelings and revels in the blessing of being together with his brothers, allowing his memories to guide his actions but not to control his future, all the while fulfilling the *mitzvah* of burying his father.

We are blessed by memories. We remember for old time's sake, for auld lang syne. We appreciate the blessings we had, those we have today, and those that are yet to be. We use our past to understand our present and look forward to the future.

Should old acquaintance be forgot and never brought to mind? No. Old acquaintances should not be forgot. In fact, they should be remembered, often. If possible, we should meet again and count the blessings given to us by memory. A blessing for old time's sake. A blessing for auld lang syne.

My Family, My Self

Rabbi Matthew D. Gewirtz

I have had the chance to spend a lot of time with my family as of late. Looking back, the time was wonderful, but after each experience I was exhausted. I couldn't quite figure out what it was that tired me out, until I heard reports from congregants and friends returning from their own family celebrations. I was acutely aware this year of so many who spoke about the intense and exhausting nature of spending a few days with their families. It's astounding sometimes to realize that few other relationships possess the power than that of family; familial relationships of any kind can make all of us, despite our age, feel like we did as children.

As we come to the conclusion of the Book of Genesis, we have read mainly about the story of Joseph revealing himself to his brothers. After 22 years of separation, after Joseph's juvenile and arrogant treatment of his siblings, and of course their selling of their own flesh and blood into slavery, Joseph's brothers now are sent by their father to seek food in Egypt during a time of famine. Joseph, now Pharaoh's second in command, is no longer recognizable to his brothers.

Joseph's powerful words, "I am your brother Joseph," have always moved me to tears. But not until fairly recently did I confront what perhaps is an unresolved mystery in the tale. Joseph says *Ha'od avi hai?*" immediately afterwards, and these three words form a question that opens the door to what may be a better understanding of Joseph.

Literally, these words mean, "Is my father still alive?" Joseph seems to ask the question because he wants to know Jacob's status. That is the way the majority of the traditional translators and many modern scholars understood it. But this rendition is problematic, for Joseph already knew that Jacob was still alive (Gen. 43:27).

Some of the traditional commentators, realizing this discrepancy, see in the question Joseph's amazement that his father, with all the troubles he had to endure, has not died as yet. They see Joseph's question as a rhetorical exclamation, meaning "Is he really still alive?" And some of the newer translations of the Bible have in fact picked up on this by translating these words as, "Is my father still well?" Thus, this modified translation seems to resolve the discrepancy in the text.

For me, there still seems to be more to Joseph's question. Why, after he rose from being a slave to be Pharaoh's right hand, did he never get in touch with his father? Why did Joseph not let him know that he was not only alive, but was now one of the most powerful men in the region? What son would not inform his father that he had done so well? Joseph must have had powerful personal reasons for his neglect. The Torah is silent about the matter, as are most rabbinic commentators. But there is another answer, and it is found in Joseph's challenged experience as a youth in his father's house, which in his adult years caused him to avoid any contact with his parent.

Joseph was raised by his widowed father as a substitute for Rachel, the boy's mother. Jacob dressed him in a *k'tonet passim*, a fancy garment of some sort, which has been dubbed an "Amazing Technicolor Dreamcoat."[1] Was it a robe to feminize him? Is the midrash not telling us something significant when, commenting on Joseph's good looks, it said that he painted his eyes, put on blush, and walked with mincing steps? Is it possible that Joseph was doing what was needed to gain his father's approval? His father kept him at home, preventing him from working with his brothers. We can imagine that Joseph hated everything about it, and that his early dreams were an expression of his frustrations. Once away from home Joseph suppressed it all and, though as Vice-Pharaoh he could have contacted his father, he failed to do so.

Ha'od avi hai? "Is my father still alive?" was a question directed more to himself than to his brothers. He may have been asking: Is my father still living…living in the manner that hurt me so? Is my father, even with all my power, still able to control me? When Joseph reveals himself to his brothers, he perhaps comes to terms not only with them but also with his blurred relationship with his father.

When we look into the faces of those in our own families, so many of us see Joseph. We come back from family vacations or holiday get-togethers and understand in a very real way the power of familial relationships. We know from reading the Torah narrative that Joseph is clearly Jacob's favorite. Yet Jacob, to console himself from his own loss of Rachel, uses Joseph, somehow placing him into the role of his wife. Joseph paid for his father's love, and then when he was successful in his own right, he was not sure if he would fall right back into his childhood role.

We, too, because of the natural vulnerability of family relationships, have been put or have put our loved ones in similar situations. We, too, have had to pay for love or for parental or family approval, or have been charged a heavy emotional price for the same. The connection to family carries with it the power to cause profound pain or ultimate fulfillment. The question, of course, is how we choose to use that power. Many of us have been hurt, and we know well that reconciliation is not always easy or readily achieved. However, we all have the opportunity to sort out what we need to do to resolve our own pain and what we can do to empower others to be independent, yet still be part of the family. When those goals are achieved, we then have the possibility of functional dependence, for parents, for children, for spouses, and for siblings.

Now I have the blessing of spending half an hour a week with first graders, teaching them Torah, helping them understand and experience the peaceful and wondrous nature of Shabbat. It is natural for me to tell them how proud I am of them when they reach new heights in their learning. I notice that they now yearn for that approval when I am with them. But one of the best pieces of learning I have done here as a rabbi came from one of my colleagues in the religious school. She told me it is wonderful that you always tell the children how proud you are of them, but it would also be helpful if you tell them how proud they must be of themselves. She went on to explain that we have the power to train our children to learn to be proud in their own right for achievements gained. If praise primarily comes from those with power, our children will grow up constantly trying to please and not build their own sense of self.

Ha'od avi hai? Joseph asks. Will my father still live his life in the way in which he did when I was a child? Will he still have the overriding power that makes me feel like a kid? We all ask Joseph's question. We all have significant power in our relationships with family. We need to acknowledge that power but also remember the importance of seeing those around us as made in the image of God...especially when they are family. May we all have the strength to know that our relationships are not about easy reconciliation, but about knowing each day that we have the potential to change, to reconnect, and to establish loving and healthy relationships that are worthy of blessing.

---

[1] *Joseph and the Amazing Technicolor Dreamcoat* is a musical by composer Andrew Lloyd Webber and lyricist Tim Rice, first performed in 1970.

Who Are These?

Stuart Tauber

As the book of Genesis comes to a close, we find Jacob preparing to bless his children before he passes on. In Egypt, life for the family has been fruitful. In his heart, however, Jacob knows the good life eventually will take a turn for the worse and lead to great suffering. His blessings will be meant to bind the family together to ensure their ultimate survival in the face of future challenges. Included in those blessings will be his grandchildren, Ephraim and Menashe, whom Jacob will bless as if they are his own children.

As part of the tale, Joseph comes to visit Jacob, bringing along with him Ephraim and Menashe, his children. Noticing them off to the side Jacob asks Joseph, "Who are these (children)?" Joseph replies "They are my sons." Biblical scholars have always found this interaction to be quite puzzling. They wonder: Is this the first time Jacob is meeting his grandchildren? (Why else wouldn't he recognize them?) Has Joseph not brought them around to meet Jacob during their grandfather's entire stay in Egypt? (Surely, he must have.) Are Jacob's eyes and senses failing, as the Torah notes, so badly? (Is that why he doesn't recognize his own grandchildren?)

The general consensus appears to be that Jacob did indeed know them. He clearly recognized the grandchildren he had been meeting with on a regular basis. This has led many scholars to believe that with the question "Who are these?," Jacob is instead looking for an answer with a deeper meaning.

You see, Ephraim and Menashe were different from the other members of the family. They were not raised under the influence of Jacob alongside his family of Hebraic faith. No, these children were raised in the Pharaoh's courtyard with a father who served as the Vice Pharaoh. They did not dress, speak, or act like the rest of the family. They dressed, spoke, and acted like Egyptian royalty. Unlike the rest of the family, who had been born in the land of Israel, they were born in the Diaspora. All things being equal, Joseph's children could have been part of a long-standing Jewish joke: "You're Jewish? Funny, you don't look Jewish."

In many ways the children of Joseph are similar to 21st-century American Jews. Like the Jewish citizens living in the modern-day Jewish state, we too are remnants of the Jewish community exiled from Israel during the destruction of the Temple in 586 BCE. However, unlike the Israeli-born Sabras, most of today's American Jews were born and raised in the Diaspora. While we are all, poetically speaking, brothers and sisters, we may not be very much alike. Most American Jews don't speak Hebrew. Although we all dress in modern styles, most American Jews are not wearing military uniforms, as are many Israelis as they protect God's chosen land. So we need to ask ourselves, are we really still brothers and sisters? Are we really still one people, one Jewish nation?

And that precisely was Jacob's dilemma. "Who are these?" Are these grandchildren of mine still part of God's chosen people, or have they become so assimilated that in a crowd we wouldn't even know they were Jewish? Will my blessing to them be a curse to the Jewish people of the future? Are they still linked to my other children? In fact, one biblical legend has it that having been granted the power of prophecy by God, Jacob knew for a fact that the future descendants of Ephraim and Menashe would be idolators and lead the Jewish people to abandon the ways of God.

And so Joseph answers the question for him: "These are my sons." In other words, you don't have to worry. Yes, they look different, but I have made sure that they know from where they come. They know their roots. While there will be moments in the future when they may stumble – just as the future descendants of your other children will – in the end you can count on them to remember that they are part of the great nation that you have fathered. In that case, an assured Jacob responds, saying "bring them to me," and I will bless them accordingly.

As *Parashat Vayehi* and the book of Genesis come to an end, the Torah once again leaves us with a great message. There will be times when we are challenged to recognize members of our own Jewish family. Their styles of dress, speech, life choices, and decisions may all seem foreign to us. At that moment, when we are feeling perplexed and asking ourselves "who are these?," we need to recall the answer of Joseph that "these are my sons." More importantly we should heed as well the words of our forefather Jacob, "then I shall treat them as my sons," in the hope that all Jews will treat one another as family, keeping us strong enough to face the challenges that will accompany our destiny.

Glossary

Aron kodesh – Holy Ark

B'rakha– a blessing

Beshert – a soulmate or predestined spouse

Bikur ḥolim – visiting the sick

Brit milah – a ceremony, as a sign of the covenant with God, at which a male Jewish child is circumcised eight days after his birth

Chutzpah – audacity, boldness

D'var Torah – a written or spoken insight on Torah; literally "words of Torah"

Halakha – Jewish law

Haran – a place mentioned in the Torah, widely believed to be in present-day Turkey

Hashem – a representative name of God; literally "The Name"

Ḥasidism – a Jewish movement with an emphasis on serving God with joy that began in Eastern Europe in the 1700s as an alternative to the emphasis on rigorous scholarship of traditional Jewish texts.

Ḥumash – the Five Books of Moses which comprise the first section of the Hebrew Bible

Ḥuppah – wedding canopy

Melakhim – angels; messengers of God

Mentsch – a fine and honorable person, one with integrity and noble values

Midrash – commentaries and interpretations by the rabbinic sages on biblical texts

Mitzvah – a religious obligation (plural: *mitzvot*)

Neshama – soul

Ohel – tent

Parasha – the weekly Torah reading (plural: *parashiyot*)

Peshat – the most basic interpretation of Torah text

Shaḥarit – morning prayer service

Shekalim – plural of *shekel*, an ancient monetary unit; modern Israeli currency

Shul – Yiddish word for synagogue

Tefillah – prayer

Tefillin – small leather boxes that contain biblical passages written on parchment; each box has long leather straps so the boxes may be worn on the forehead and on one arm.

Tikkun olam – repairing the world; social action

Torah – *See ḥumash*; also a reference to traditional Jewish texts and commentaries on them.

Tzedekah – an act of justice, righteousness; the obligation to perform an act of charity

Tzadik – a righteous person

Contributors

Rabbi Scott Aaron was the rabbinic intern for Hofstra Hillel from 1993 to 1996. He has spent most of his career since then working with Jewish Emerging Adults, including writing two guidebooks on how to live meaningful Jewish lives on campus, and his PhD dissertation on gauging the impact of experiences such as Birthright Israel and Alternative Spring Break trips on Jewish identity. Scott credits this career path in large part to his Hofstra Hillel experience and his role model, Rabbi Mitelman. He also credits Rabbi Mitelman for his wonderful family because Scott met his wife, Rabbi Donni Aaron, while she was also working part-time at Hofstra Hillel.

Loen Amer served as the Wohl Family Engagement Coordinator at Hofstra Hillel from 2011 to 2012. She has been an experiential Jewish educator working with teens since she was one herself. She is the Director of Youth Engagement at Bet Torah in Mt. Kisco, New York. Before joining the Bet Torah family, she was the Marketing and Recruitment Coordinator for Ramah Israel of the National Ramah Commission. Loen previously worked with teens at two Conservative congregations on Long Island: Beth Sholom in Roslyn Heights and the Woodbury Jewish Center. She also volunteered as the Education Coordinator for the Rakevet Division of METNY USY.

Loen has a voracious love for life-long Jewish learning and most recently studied *Torah le'shmah*, Torah for its own sake, at the Conservative Yeshiva in Jerusalem. She also studied at Gratz College, Columbia University, and the Jewish Theological Seminary. Loen lives on Manhattan's Upper West Side and enjoys baking and reading.

Rabbi Dr. Ronald L. Androphy is spiritual leader of the East Meadow Jewish Center, a position he has held for the past 33 years. He is also an adjunct professor at the Jewish Theological Seminary. A native of Waterbury, Connecticut, Rabbi Androphy received his BA in economics from Brandeis University and his Masters degree, rabbinic ordination, DHL in Bible and an honorary DD from the Jewish Theological Seminary (JTS). He and his congregation have always welcomed Hofstra students on the High Holy Days and Shabbat.

Rabbi Daniel Bar-Nahum is the rabbi and educator at Temple Emanu-El of East Meadow, a congregation which began a strategic partnership with Hofstra Hillel in 2014. Temple Emanu-El opens its doors to Hofstra students on Rosh Hashanah, Yom Kippur and, of course, on Shabbat. Rabbi Bar-Nahum was ordained in 2012 by Hebrew Union College – Jewish Institute of Religion in New York.

Elias Chajet graduated in 2015 from Hofstra University, where he majored in Jewish Studies. During his time at Hofstra, Elias became active in Hofstra Hillel and in Greek life, serving as President of Sigma Alpha Mu for two years. He also worked at Temple Beth-El of Great Neck, New York, as a Hebrew teacher, tutor, and family educator. Elias then worked as an Education Fellow for the Institute of Southern Jewish life, traveling around the South working with religious schools. Elias is now studying in Jerusalem in his first year of rabbinical school at Hebrew Union College – Jewish Institute of Religion.

Rabbi Matthew D. Gewirtz began his tenure as the Senior Rabbi of Congregation B'nai Jeshurun in Short Hills, New Jersey, in July 2006. Previously he served as Senior Associate Rabbi of Congregation Rodeph Sholom in New York City. In 1996 he earned his Masters in Hebrew Literature from Hebrew Union College-Jewish Institute of Religion where he was ordained in 1997.

Rabbi Gewirtz has appeared on numerous television programs, including *Morning Joe*. He is a prolific writer and author and now is actively involved with the Newark Interfaith Coalition for Hope and Peace. He states his most important connection with Hofstra Hillel is how much he has always admired and looked up to Rabbi Mitelman.

Rabbi Fred Greene was a Political Science and Jewish Studies major at Hofstra University in the class of 1992. He was ordained by the Hebrew Union College – Jewish Institute of Religion and is the rabbi at Congregation Har HaShem of Boulder, Colorado. Among his fondest memories are his visits with Rabbi Meir Mitelman in the Hofstra Hillel office and the endless supply of Stella D'Oro cookes.

Rabbi Andrew Jacobs has been the spiritual leader of Ramat Shalom Synagogue in Fort Lauderdale, Florida, since 2002. He was the Program Director at Hofstra Hillel from 1992 to 1993. Rabbi Jacobs is a graduate of Vassar College, holds a Masters of Arts in Jewish Art and Material Culture from the Jewish Theological Seminary in consortium with Columbia University and the Jewish Museum of New York. He was ordained by the Reconstructionist Rabbinical College. He maintains a blog (rabbiandrewjacobs.org) and a website (findyourish.com). Rabbi Jacobs and his wife, Rabbi Cheryl Jacobs, are the proud parents of Abigail and Jonah.

Rabbi David Kalb is the rabbi of the Jewish Learning Center of New York (www.jewishlearningcenterny.org). He is a member of the Jewish Religious Equality Coalition at the American Jewish Committee, an associate faculty member of CLAL: The National Jewish Center for Learning and Leadership, and a Senior Rabbinic Fellow at the Shalom Hartman Institute. Rabbi Kalb served on the educational advisory board of the WNET/BBC documentary, *The Story of the Jews*, and has taught Jewish Studies classes at Hofstra Hillel.

He received his BA through the joint program at Columbia University/Jewish Theological Seminary, and received his rabbinic ordination from Rabbi Shlomo Riskin, Rosh Hayeshiva of Yeshivat Hamivtar in Efrat. Rabbi Kalb also has studied at Hebrew University and the Shalom Hartman Institute.

Rabbi Yehuda Kelemer is the spiritual leader of Young Israel of West Hempstead, New York. He is the *Rav Hamachshir* (Certifying Rabbi) at Eli's Kosher Kitchen, the kosher eatery at Hofstra University.

Bruce A. Lev currently serves as the Chair of Hofstra Uiversity Hillel's Board of Trustees. He has a long, active affiliation with Hillel since participating as a student officer of Hillel in the early 1980s. Bruce has a passion for Hillel's vision of "having every Jewish student make an enduring commitment to Jewish life, learning, and Israel." He extends that passion beyond the college campus to the Jewish community at large and welcomes others to join him in this vision of all Jewish adults making a similar commitment – regardless of background – to a meaningful Jewish life, learning, and Israel.

Gittel Marcus attended Hofstra University from 1997 to 2000 and graduated with a BA in Jewish Studies. While at Hofstra, she served on the Hillel board. She currently lives in Israel with her husband and four daughters. Her first book, *Night Tales of Meron Mountain*, is currently available at major online book stores.

Bob Margulies is a lawyer living in West Hempstead, New York, and is active in the Jewish community. He attended Hofstra University (1975-1979), graduating with a BBA in Accounting. While at Hofstra, Bob and his close friends were very involved in Hofstra Hillel for all four years, leading programs which catapulted Hillel into a regional Hillel presence. Bob was instrumental in bringing Rabbi Meir Mitelman to Adelphi University Hillel first and, eight years later, to Hofstra Hillel. Bob is proud that he has had a friendship with Rabbi Mitelman for more than 40 years and is honored that Rabbi Mitelman officiated at Bob's wedding to Gila in 1984.

Rabbi Meir Mitelman (aka Rabs) received his rabbinic ordination and MS in Jewish Education in 1977 from Yeshiva University (YU). He also holds an MSW from YU's Wurzweiler School of Social Work, conferred in 1982.

Rabs began his Hillel career at Adelphi University in 1977. From 1985 through 2008, he was the Executive Director at Hofstra Hillel and continues to serve Hofstra Hillel in myriad ways. He is also a Hofstra faculty member. Rabbi Meir was the 2005 Hofstra SGA Advisor of the Year and was honored by UJA-Federation of New York/Long Island office in 2006 with the Jewish Educator award. One of his greatest joys is his ongoing relationships with his students and their children throughout the decades.

Rabbi Michael Paley is the Pearl and Ira Meyer Scholar in Residence at UJA-Federation of New York. He has also been the University Chaplain at Columbia University and was the founding Director of the Edgar M. Bronfman Youth Fellowship in Israel. His first position was as the Associate Chaplain and Hillel Director at Dartmouth College where he met and was befriended by a very much younger Rabbi Meir Mitelman. Through his work with the Wexner Heritage Foundation he has had the distinct pleasure of teaching many members of the Board of Hofstra Hillel.

Rabbi Noam Raucher was born in southern Connecticut to a warm and loving family. He is a proud graduate of Hofstra University (2002) — go Pride! Throughout his time at Hofstra, Noam remembers interesting classes, great times with friends, and the deep wisdom found only in the Hillel offices on campus. Currently he serves as Senior Rabbi at the Pasadena Jewish Temple and Center in Pasadena, California. He enjoys hiking, biking, fish tacos, and spending time with his partner, Tamar, and their two boys, Judah and Elijah.

Rabbi Lyle Rothman joined the University of Miami Hillel team as Campus Rabbi and Jewish Chaplain in July 2016. He was ordained and received his MA in Religious Education from Hebrew Union College-JIR in 2012. Rabbi Lyle graduated from Hofstra University in 2004 and returned to Hofstra Hillel as a rabbinic intern, later serving as its Director of Jewish Life and Learning. He received the first Alumnus of the Year award at Hofstra Hillel's 65th anniversary dinner. Rabbi Lyle is passionately dedicated to interdenomi-national and interfaith work and has been known to smile incessantly when talking about the Jewish calendar.

Rabbi Bruce Bromberg Seltzer currently serves as Hillel Director and Jewish Advisor at Amherst College, teaches at Western New England University, and works at Camp Ramah New England. He worked as a rabbinic intern at Hofstra Hillel during the 1999-2000 academic year before being ordained by the Jewish Theological Seminary in May 2000. He has also worked at Duke University and Smith College. Rabbi Bruce lives in Northampton, Massachusetts, with his wife and four children.

Rabbi Dave Siegel has been the Executive Director of Hofstra University Hillel since 2011. Throughout his career, he has focused on issues of leadership and professional development in the Jewish community. In addition to rabbinic ordination from the Jewish Theological Seminary, he has received Masters degrees from both New York University's Robert F. Wagner Graduate School of Public Service and JTS's William Davidson Graduate School of Jewish Education.

Dave has served in leadership positions at the 92nd Street Y, Camp Ramah in the Berkshires, the Foundation for Jewish Camp, and United Synagogue Youth (USY). In addition to his work with Hofstra Hillel, he is pursuing his doctorate in Educational Leadership from JTS.

Stuart Tauber is the Vice President of UJA-Federation of New York, overseeing the Long Island region. He has had the pleasure of working with the wonderful rabbis and lay leaders dedicated to the Jewish student community of Hofstra University Hillel. As a past Hillel student president, he is well aware of how many young adults take the first steps in their lifelong Jewish journeys at the local Hillel. In the case of Hofstra Hillel, these particular students have been blessed with exceptional caring and loving leadership for so many years under the divinely inspired wings of Rabbi Meir Mitelman and now Rabbi Dave Siegel.

Rabbi Daniel Treiser served as an Outreach Fellow for Hofstra University Hillel from 1994 to 1995. In addition to supporting Jewish life programming on campus, he focused on promoting Israel experience programs for Jewish students. He is the rabbi of Temple B'nai Israel in Clearwater, Florida. He is married to Rachel Levine Treiser (Hofstra, 1996), whom he first met working on an intercollegiate Hillel event between Hofstra and Queens College Hillel in 1993.

Micah Guerin Weiss holds a BA in Religion and in African American Studies from Wesleyan University. Micah currently is a student at the Reconstructionist Rabbinical College. Previously, Micah worked as the Leadership Coach and Rabbinic Consultant at J-Teen Leadership in Westchester, New York, and taught Jewish Ethics and Judaism at Mechon Hadar and Social Justice at Hofstra Hillel. Micah serves as the volnteer director of Project Hayyei Sarah, a network of emerging Jewish leaders teaching Torah about the violation of human dignity in Hebron. Micah was a fellow at Yeshivat Hadar for two years and a participant in AVODAH, the Jewish Service Corps.

Rabbi Rachel Wiesenberg is the Rabbi-Educator of Temple Beth Torah in Melville, New York. She has served as the Family Life Programmer of the Shelter Rock Jewish Center in Roslyn and as the student rabbi for the North Fork Reform Synagogue in Cutchogue, New York. Rabbi Wiesenberg received her BA in Jewish Studies from Hofstra University (2004), where she served on the executive boards of Hillel, the Jewish-Greek Council, and Delta Phi Epsilon International Sorority. She received rabbinic ordination from Hebrew Union College – Jewish Institute of Religion in 2009. Raised in Milford, Connecticut, she lives in Merrick, New York, with her husband, Jonathan (Hofstra 2003), their sons, Hunter and Reed, and their "dog-ter" Rally.

Hanita Wishnevski (HW) is a former car service driver, chess columnist, restaurant reviewer, past and present collector of miscellaneous knowle mostly as Assistant Director while Rabbi Meir Mitelman was Executive Director and University Jewish Chaplain. Admitted to the inaugural evening class of Hofstra Law School, HW received her JD and passed the Bar in 2008. Since 2009, she has worked as an attorney. To date, HW has not prosecuted (nor, *chas v'shalom*, defended) any "Word Crimes."

Mission

Hillel's mission is to enrich the lives of Jewish students
so that they may enrich the Jewish people and the world.

Vision

Hillel envisions a world in which every Jewish student
makes an enduring commitment to Jewish life, learning and Israel.

Sponsorship

Help Hofstra Hillel further its mission and vision by becoming
a sponsor for the Many Voices, One People Torah project.
Sponsor one or more essays, an entire *parasha*, or a complete book
for Exodus, Leviticus, Numbers, and Deuteronomy.

For sponsorship details, visit www.hofstrahillel.org
or email hillel@hofstra.edu.

Thank you!

CPSIA information can be obtained
at www.ICGtesting.com
Printed in the USA
FSHW04n0154210418
47081FS

ISBN 978-1-7322104-1-7

9 781732 210417